PUBLIC LIBRARIES

IN THE

UNITED STATES OF AMERICA

THEIR

HISTORY, CONDITION, AND MANAGEMENT

SPECIAL REPORT

DEPARTMENT OF THE INTERIOR, BUREAU OF EDUCATION

PART II

WASHINGTON
GOVERNMENT PRINTING OFFICE
1876

RULES

FOR A PRINTED

DICTIONARY CATALOGUE

BY

CHARLES A. CUTTER
LIBRARIAN OF THE BOSTON ATHENÆUM

PREFATORY NOTE.

There are plenty of treatises on classification, of which accounts may be found in Edwards's Memoirs of Libraries and Petzholdt's Bibliotheca Bibliographica. The classification of the St. Louis Public School Library Catalogue is briefly defended by W. T. Harris in the preface (which is reprinted, with some additions, from the Journal of Speculative Philosophy for 1869). Professor Abbot's plan is explained in a pamphlet printed and in use at Harvard College Library, also in his "Statement respecting the New Catalogue" (part of the report of the examining committee of the library for 1863), and in the North American Review for January, 1869. The plan of Mr. Schwartz, librarian of the Apprentices' Library, New York, is partially set forth in the preface to his catalogue; and a fuller explanation is preparing for publication. For an author-catalogue there are the famous 91 rules of the British Museum* (prefixed to the Catalogue of Printed Books, Vol. 1, 1841, or conveniently arranged in alphabetical order by Th. Nichols in his Handbook for Readers at the British Museum, 1866); Prof. Jewett's modification of them (Smithsonian Report on the Construction of Catalogues, 1852); Mr. F. B. Perkins's further modification (in the American Publisher for 1869), and a chapter in the second volume of Edwards. But for a dictionary catalogue as a whole, and for most of its parts, there is no manual whatever. Nor have any of the above-mentioned works attempted to set forth the rules in a systematic way or to investigate what might be called the first principles of cataloguing. It is to be expected that a first attempt will be incomplete, and I shall be obliged to librarians for criticisms, objections, or new problems, with or without solutions. With such assistance perhaps a second edition of these hints would deserve the title—Rules.

* Compiled by a committee of five, Panizzi, Th. Watts, J. Winter Jones, J. H. Parry, and E. Edwards, in several months of hard labor.

CONTENTS.

General remarks.
  Objects.
  Means.
  Definitions (with a note on classification).

A. ENTRY. (Where to enter.)
  1. Author-catalogue 17
    A. Authors.
      1. Personal.
        a. Who is to be considered author.
        b. What part of the name is to be used.
        c. What form of the name is to be used.
      2. Corporate.
    B. Substitutes for authors.
    C. References.
    D. Economies.
  2. Title-catalogue 32
  3. Subject-catalogue 37
    A. Entries considered separately.
      1. Choice between different subjects.
      2. Choice between different names.
    B. Entries considered as parts of a whole.
  4. Form-catalogue 49
  5. Analysis 52

B. STYLE. (How to enter.) 52
  1. Headings.
  2. Titles. (Abridgement, etc.)
  3. Editions.
  4. Imprints.
  5. Contents and notes.
  6. References.
  7. Capitals.
  8. Punctuation, etc.
    a. Headings.
    b. Titles.
    c. Editions.
    d. Imprints.
  9. Arrangement.

RULES

FOR A

DICTIONARY CATALOGUE.

No code of cataloguing could be adopted in all points by everyone, because the libraries for study and the libraries for reading have different objects, and those which combine the two do so in different proportions. Again, the preparation of a catalogue must vary as it is to be manuscript or printed, and, if the latter, as it is to be merely an index to the library, giving in the shortest possible compass clues by which the public can find books, or is to attempt to furnish more information on various points, or finally is to be made with a certain regard to what may be called style. Without pretending to exactness we may divide dictionary catalogues into short-title, medium-title, and full-title or bibliographic; typical examples of the three being, 1°, the Boston Mercantile (1869) or the Cincinnati Public (1871); 2°, the Boston Public (1861 and 1866) or the Boston Athenæum (1872); 3°, the author-part of the Congress (1869) and the Surgeon General's (1872–'74) or least abridged of any, the present card catalogue of the Boston Public Library. To avoid the constant repetition of such phrases as "the full catalogue of a large library" and "a concise finding-list," I shall use the three words Short, Medium, and Full as proper names, with the preliminary caution that the Short family are not all of the same size, that there is more than one Medium, and that Full may be Fuller and Fullest. Short, if single-columned, is generally a title-a-liner; if printed in double columns, it allows the title occasionally to exceed one line, but not, if possible, two; Medium does not limit itself in this way, but it seldom exceeds four lines, and gets many titles into a single line. Full usually fills three or four lines and often takes six or seven for a title.

The number of the following rules is not owing to any complexity of system, but to the number of cases to which a few simple principles have to be applied. They are especially designed for Medium, but may easily be adapted to Short by excision and marginal notes. The almost universal practice of printing the shelf-numbers renders some of them unnecessary for town and city libraries.

OBJECTS.

1. To enable a person to find a book of which either
   - (A) the author ⎫
   - (B) the title ⎬ is known.
   - (C) the subject ⎭
2. To show what the library has
   - (D) by a given author
   - (E) on a given subject
   - (F) in a given kind of literature.
3. To assist in the choice of a book
   - (G) as to its edition (bibliographically).
   - (H) as to its character (literary or topical).

MEANS.

1. Author-entry with the necessary references (for A and D).
2. Title-entry or title-reference (for B).
3. Subject-entry, cross-references, and classed subject-table (for C and E).
4. Form-entry* (for F).
5. Giving edition and imprint, with notes when necessary (for G).
6. Notes (for H).

DEFINITIONS.

There is such confusion in the use of terms in the various prefaces to catalogues, — a confusion that at once springs from and leads to confusion of thought and practice, — that it is worth while to propose a systematic nomenclature.

Analysis. See *Reference, Analytical.*

Anonymous, published without the author's name.

Strictly a book is not anonymous if the author's name appears anywhere in it, but it is safest to treat it as anonymous if the author's name does not appear in the title.

Asyndetic, without cross references. See *Syndetic.*

Author, in the narrower sense, is the person who writes a book; in a wider sense it may be applied to him who is the cause of the book's existence by putting together the writings of several authors (usually called *the editor*, more properly to be called *the collector*). Bodies of men (societies, cities, legislative bodies, countries) are to be considered the authors of their memoirs, transactions, journals, debates, reports, &c.

Class, a collection of objects having characteristics in common.

Books are classified by bringing together those which have the same characteristics.† Of course any characteristics might be taken, as size, or binding, or publisher. But as nobody wants to know what books there are in the library in folio, or what quartos, or what books bound in russia or calf, or what published by John Smith, or by Brown, Jones, and Robinson, these bases of classification are left to the booksellers and auctioneers and trade sales. Still, in

---

* Here the whole is designated by its most important member. The full name would be form-and-language entry. Kind-entry would not suggest the right idea.

† This note has grown out of some epistolary controversy. It has little direct bearing on practice, but by its insertion here some one interested in the theory of cataloguing may be saved the trouble of going over the same ground.

case of certain unusual or noted bindings, as human skin or Grolier's, or early or famous publishers, as Aldus and Elzevir, a partial class-list is sometimes very properly made. But books are most commonly brought together in catalogues because they have the same authors, or the same subjects, or the same literary form, or are written in the same language, or were given by the same donor, or are designed for the same class of readers. When brought together because they are by the same author they are not usually thought of as classified; they form the author-catalogue, and need no further mention here except in regard to arrangement. The classes, *i. e.* in this case the authors, might of course be further classified according to their nations, or their professions (as the subjects are in national or professional biographies) or by any other set of common characteristics, but for library purposes an alphabetical arrangement according to the spelling of their names is universally acknowledged to be the best.

The classification by language is not generally used in full. There are catalogues in which all the English books are separated from all the foreign; in others there are separate lists of French books or German books. The needs of each library must determine whether it is worth while to prepare such lists. It is undeniably useful in almost any library to make lists of the belles lettres in the different languages; which though nominally a classification by language is really a classification by literary form, the object being to bring together all the works with a certain national flavor,—the French flavor, the German flavor. Again, it is useful to give lists not of the belles lettres alone but of all the works in the rarer languages, as the Bodleian and the British Museum have published separate lists of their Hebrew books. Here too the circumstances of each library must determine where it shall draw the line between those literatures which it will put by themselves and those which it will include and hide in the mass of its general catalogue. Note, however, that some of the difficulties of transliterating names of modern Greek, Russian authors, &c., are removed by putting their original works in a separate catalogue, though translations still remain to puzzle us.

The catalogue by donors or original owners is usually partial (as those of the Dowse, Barton, Prince, and Ticknor libraries). The catalogues by classes of readers are also partial, hardly extending beyond **Juvenile literature** and **Sunday-school books**. Of course many subject classes amount to the same thing, the class **Medicine** being especially useful to medical men, **Theology** to the theologians, and so on.

Classification by subject and classification by form are the most common. An example will best show the distinction between them. **Theology**, which is itself a subject, is also a class, that is, it is extensive enough to have its parts, its chapters, so to speak (as **Future Life, Holy Spirit, Regeneration, Sin, Trinity**), treated separately, each when so treated (whether in books or only in thought) being itself a subject; all these together, inasmuch as they possess this in common, that they have to do with some part of the relations of God to man, form the class of subjects **Theology**. Class, however, is applied to **Poetry** in a different sense. It then signifies not a collection of similar subjects but a collection of books resembling one another in being composed in that form and with that spirit, whatever it is, which is called poetical. In the subject-catalogue class is used in the first sense,—collection of similar subjects; in the form-catalogue it is used in the second,—list of similar books.

Most systems of classification are mixed, as the following analysis of one in actual use in a small library will show:

Art, science, and natural history.	*Subj.*
History and biography.	*Subj.*
Poetry.	*Form* (literary).
Encyclopædias and books of reference.	*Form* (practical).
Travels and adventures.	*Subj.* (Has some similarity to a Form-class.)
Railroads.	*Subj.*
Fiction.	*Form.* (*Novels*, a sub-division of *Fiction*, is properly a Form-class; but the differentia of the more extensive class *Fiction* is not its form, but its untruth; imaginary voyages and the like of course imitate the form of the works which they parody.)
Relating to the rebellion.	*Subj.*
Magazines.	*Form* (practical)
General literature, essays, and religious works.	A mixture: 1. Hardly a class; that is to say, it probably is a collection of books having only this in common, that they will not fit into any of the other classes; 2. *Form;* 3. *Subj.*

Confining ourselves now to classification by subjects the word can be used in three senses:

1. Bringing books together which treat of the same subject specifically.
   That is books which each treat of the whole of the subject and not of a part only.
2. Bringing books together which treat of similar subjects.
   Or, to express the same thing differently:
   Bringing subjects together so as to form a class.
   A catalogue so made is called a classed catalogue.
3. Bringing classes together so as to form a system.
   A catalogue so made should be called a systematic catalogue.

The three steps are then

1. Classifying the books to make subject-lists.
2. Classifying the subject-lists to make classes.
3. Classifying the classes to make a systematic catalogue.

The dictionary stops in its entries at the first stage, in its cross-references at the second.
The alphabetico-classed catalogue stops at the second stage.
The systematic alone advances to the third.

Classification in the first sense, it is plain, is the same as "entry;" in the second sense it is the same as "class-entry;" and in the third sense it is the same as the "logical arrangement" of the table on p. 13, under "Classed catalogue."

It is worth while to ascertain the relation of subject and class in the subject-catalogue. *Subject* is the matter on which the author is seeking to give or the reader to obtain information; *Class* is, as said above, a grouping of subjects which have characteristics in common. A little reflection will show that the words so used partially overlap,* the general subjects being classes† and the classes being subjects,‡ but the individual subjects§ never being classes.

Class-entry, registering a book under the name of its class; in the subject-catalogue used in contradistinction to specific entry.

E. g. a book on repentance has class entry under **Theology**; its specific entry would be under **Repentance.**

Classed catalogues are made by class-entry, whether the classes so formed are arranged logically as in the Systematic kind or alphabetically as in the Alphabetico-classed.

A dictionary catalogue contains class-headings, inasmuch as it contains the headings of extensive subjects, but under them there is no class entry, only specific entry. The syndetic dictionary catalogue, however, recognizes their nature by its cross-references, which constitute it in a certain degree an alphabetico-classed (not a systematic) catalogue. Moreover the dictionary catalogue, without ceasing to be one, might, if it were thought worth while (which it certainly is not), not merely give titles under specific headings but repeat them

* 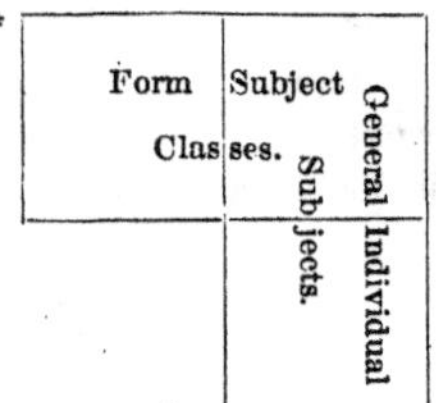

† The subjects **Animals, Horses, Plants,** are classes, a fact which is perhaps more evident to the eye if we use the terms **Zoology, Hippology, Botany.** The subdivisions of **Botany** and **Zoology** are obvious enough; the subdivisions of **Hippology** may be themselves classes, as **Shetland ponies, Arabian coursers, Barbs,** or individual horses, as **Lady Suffolk, Justin Morgan.**

‡ Not merely the concrete classes **Natural history, Geography, Herpetology, History, Ichthyology, Mineralogy** but the abstract ones **Mathematics, Philosophy** are plainly subjects. The fact that some books treat of the subject **Philosophy** and others of philosophical subjects and that others treat in a philosophical manner subjects not usually considered philosophical, introduces confusion into the matter; and single examples may be brought up in which it seems as if the classification expressed the form (Crestadoro's "nature") or something which a friend calls the "essence" of the book and not its subject, so that we ought to speak of an "essence-catalogue" which might require some special treatment; but the distinction cannot be maintained. It might be said, for example, that "Geology a proof of revelation" would have for its *subject-matter* **Geology** but for its *class* **Theology,**—which is true, not because class and subject are incompatible but because this book has two subjects, the first **Geology,** the second one of the evidences of revealed religion, wherefore, as the **Evidences** are a subdivision of **Theology,** the book belongs under that as a subject-class.

§ It is plain enough that **Mt. Jefferson, John Milton,** the **Warrior Iron-clad** are not classes. Countries, however, which for most purposes it is convenient to consider as individual, are in certain aspects classes; when by the word "England" we mean "the English" it is the name of a class.

under certain classes or under all classes in ascending series, *e. g.* not merely have such headings as **Rose, Geranium, Fungi, Liliaceæ, Phænogamia, Cryptogamia,** but also under **Botany** include all the titles which appeared under **Rose, Geranium,** etc.; *provided* the headings **Botany, Cryptogamia, Fungi,** etc., were arranged alphabetically. The matter may be tabulated thus:

Arrangement	Entry	Catalogue
Alphabetical arrangement.	Specific entry. (Common dict. catal.)	Dictionary catalogue.
	Specific entry and class reference (Bost. Pub. Lib., Boston Athenæum.)	
	Specific and class entry. (No example.)	
	Class entry with specific or class subentry. (Noyes.)	Alphabetico-classed catalogue.
	Class entry with chiefly class subentry. (Abbot.)	
Logical arrangement.	Class entry. (Undivided classed catal.)	Systematic catalogue.
	Class entry and subentry and finally specific subentry. (Subdivided classed catal.)	

Alphabetical arrangement.

Single subjects.	Specific headings in alphabetical order.	Classes in alphabetical order.	Classes of subjects.
	A	B	
	D	C	
	Specific headings arranged logically in classes.	Classes in logical order.	

Logical arrangement.

A, Specific dictionary.

B, Specific dict. by its cross-references and its form-entries. Alphabetico-classed catalogue.

C, Classed catalogue without subdivisions.

D, Classed catalogue with subdivisions.

A, B are alphabetical.

C, D are classed.

A, B, D contain specific subjects.

B, C, D contain classes.

The specific entries of A and the classes of B, though brought together in the same catalogues (the class-dictionary and the alphabetico-classed) simply stand side by side and do not unite, each preserving its own nature, because the principle which brings them together—the alphabet—is external, mechanical. But in D the specific entries and the classes become intimately united to form a homogeneous whole, because the principle which brings them together—the relations of the subjects to one another—is internal, chemical, so to speak.

Collector. See *Author.*

Cross-reference. See *Reference.*

Dictionary catalogue, so called because the headings (author, title, subject, and form) are arranged, like the words in a dictionary, in alphabetical order.

Dictionary and other alphabetical catalogues. These are differentiated not, as is often said, by the dictionary having specific entry, but (1) by its giving specific entries in all cases and (2) by its individual entry.

Even the classed catalogues often have specific entry. Whenever a book treats of the whole subject of a class it is specifically entered under that class. A theological encyclopædia is specifically entered under **Theology,** and theology is an unsubordinated class in many systems. The alphabetico-classed catalogues have specific entry in many more cases, because they have many more classes. Prof. Abbot has such headings as **Ink, Jute, Lace, Leather, Life-savers, Locks, Mortars, Perfumery, Safes, Salt, Smoke, Snow, Varnish, Vitriol.** Mr. Noyes has scores of similar headings. But neither of them permits individual entry, which the dictionary catalogue requires. The alphabetico-classed catalogue enters a life of Napoleon and a history of England under **Biography** and **History**; the dictionary enters them under **Napoleon** and **England.** This is the invariable and chief distinction between the two.

Editor. See *Author.*

Entry, the registry of a book in the catalogue with the title and imprint.

Author-entry, such registry with the author's name for a heading.

Title-entry, registry under some word of the title.

First-word-entry, such entry made from the first word of the title not an article.

Important-word, or *catch-word-entry,* such entry made from some word of the title other than the first word and not indicative of the subject, but likely to be remembered and used by borrowers in asking for the book.

Subject-word-entry, such entry made under a word of the title which indicates the subject of the book.

Subject-entry, registry under the name selected by the cataloguer to indicate the subject.

A cataloguer who should put "The insect," by Michelet, under **Entomology**, would be making a *subject-entry;* Duncan's "Introduction to entomology" entered under the same head would be at once a *subject-entry* and a *subject-word-entry.*

Form-entry, registry under the name of the kind of literature to which the book belongs.

Form, applied to a variety of classification founded on the form of the book classified, which may be either *Practical,* as in **Almanacs, Dictionaries, Encyclopædias, Gazetteers, Indexes, Tables** (the form in these being for the most part alphabetical), or *Literary,* as **Fiction, Plays, Comedies, Farces, Tragedies, Poetry, Letters, Orations, Sermons** (the latter with the subdivisions Charity, Election, Funeral, Installation, Ordination, Thanksgiving, etc.). There are certain headings which belong both to the Subject and the Form family. "**Encyclopædias,**" inasmuch as the books treat of all knowledge, is the most inclusive of all the subject-classes; inasmuch as (with few exceptions) they are in alphabetic form, it is a form-class.

Heading, the word by which the alphabetical place of an entry in the catalogue is determined, usually the name of the author, of the subject, or of the literary or practical form, or a word of the title.

Imprint, the indication of the place, date, and form of printing.

Polygraphic, written by several authors.

Polytopical, treating of several topics.

Will the convenience of this word excuse the twist given to the meaning of τόπος in its formation? Polygraphic might serve, as the French use polygraphe for a miscellaneous writer; but it will be well to have both words,—*polygraphic* denoting (as now) collections of several works by one or many authors, *polytopical* denoting works on many subjects.

Reference, partial registry of a book (omitting the imprint) under author, title, subject, or kind, referring to a more full entry under some other heading; occasionally used to denote merely entries without imprints, in which the reference is implied. The distinction of entry and reference is almost without meaning for Short, as a title-a-liner saves nothing by referring unless there are several references.

Analytical-reference, or, simply, *an analytical*, the registry of some part of a book or of some work contained in a collection, referring to the heading under which the book or collection is entered.

Cross-reference, reference from one subject to another.

Heading-reference, from one form of a heading to another.

First-word-reference, *catch-word-reference*, *subject-word-reference*, same as first-word-entry, etc., omitting the imprint, and referring.

Specific entry, registering a book under a heading which expresses its special subject as distinguished from entering it in a class which includes that subject.

E. g., registering "The art of painting" under **Painting**, or a description of the cactus under **Cactus**. Putting them under **Fine arts** and **Botany** would be class-entry. "Specific entry," by the way, has nothing to do with "species."

Subject, the theme or themes of the book, whether stated in the title or not.

It is worth noting that subjects are of two sorts: (1) individual, as **Goethe, Shakespeare, England**, the **Middle Ages**, the ship **Alexandra**, the dog **Tray**, the **French Revolution**, all of which are concrete; and (2) general, as **Man, History, Horse, Philosophy**, which may be either concrete or abstract. Every general subject is a class more or less extensive. (See note on *Class*.) Some mistakes have also arisen from not noting that certain words, **Poetry, Fiction, Drama**, etc., are subject-headings for the books written about Poetry, Fiction, etc., and form-headings for poems, novels, plays, etc.

Subject-entry, *Subject-word-entry*. See *Entry*.

Syndetic, connective, applied to that kind of dictionary catalogue which binds its entries together by means of cross-references so as to form a whole, the references being made from the most comprehensive subject to those of the next lower degree of comprehensiveness, and from each of these to their subordinate subjects, and so on. These cross-references correspond to and are an imperfect substitute for the arrangement in a systematic catalogue. References are also made in the syndetic catalogue to illustrative and co-ordinate subjects.

Title in the broader sense includes heading, title proper, and imprint; in the narrower (in which it is hereinafter used) it is the name of the book given by the author on the title-page, omitting the imprint, but including names of editors, translators, etc. The name of the book put on the leaf preceding the title-page is called the *half-title;* and the same term is applied to lines indicating subdivisions of the book and following the title; the name given at the head of the first page of text is the *caption*. That given on the back of the book (the *binder's title*) should never be used in a catalogue which makes the slightest pretensions to carefulness.

A title may be either the book's name (as "&c.") or its description (as "A collection of occasional sermons"), or it may state its subject (as, "Synonyms of the New Testament") or it may be any two or all three of these combined (as, description and subject, "Brief account of a journey through Europe;" name and description, "Happy thoughts;" name and subject, "Men's wives;" all three, "Index of dates.")

Bibliographers have established a cult of the title-page; its slightest peculiarities are noted; it is followed religiously, with dots for omissions, brackets for insertions, and uprights to mark the end of lines; it is even imitated by fac-simile type or photographic copying. These things may concern the cataloguer of the Lenox Library or the Prince collection. The ordinary librarian has in general nothing to do with them; but it does not follow that even he is to lose all respect for the title. It is the book's name and should not be changed but by act of legislature. Our necessities oblige us to abbreviate it, but nothing obliges us to make additions to it or to change it without giving notice to the reader that we have done so. Moreover it must influence the entry of a book more or less; it determines the title-entry entirely; it affects the author-entry (see § 2) and the subject-entry (see § 66). But to let it have more power than this is to pay it a superstitious veneration. (§ 43, *b*)

Volume, a book distinguished from other books or other volumes of the same work by having its own title, paging, and register.

I. AUTHOR-ENTRY.

A. AUTHORS.

1. Personal.

a. Under whom as author.

Joint authors, 2, 3. Theses, 4. Pseudonyms, 5. Illustrators, 6. Musical works, 7. Booksellers and auctioneers, 8. Commentaries, 9. Continuations and indexes, 10. Concordances, 11. Reporters, translators, and editors, 12.

b. Under what part of the name.

Christian name, 13. Surname, 14. Changed names, 15. Compound names, 16. Prefixes, 17. Latin names, 18. Capes, lakes, etc., 19.

c. Under what form of the name.

Vernacular, 20. Various spellings, 21. Places, 22–24. Transliteration, 25.

2. Corporate.

General principle, 26. Places, 27. Governmental bodies, 28. Laws, 29. Works written officially, 30. Articles to be inquired after, 31. Reports, 32. Congresses, 33. Treaties, 34. Parties, denominations, orders, 35. Their conventions, conferences, etc., 36. Ecclesiastical councils, 37. Reports of committees, 38. Classes of citizens, 39. Societies, 40.

B. SUBSTITUTES.

Parts of the author's name, 41. Pseudonyms, 42. Collectors, 43.

C. REFERENCES, 44, 45.

D. ECONOMIES, 46–51.

AUTHORS.

1. Make the author-entry under (A) the name of the author whether personal or corporate, or (B) some substitute for it.

Anonymous books are to be entered under the name of the author whenever it is known.

In regard to the author-entry it must be remembered that the object is not merely to facilitate the finding of a given book by an author's name. If this were all, it might have been better to make the entry under the professed name (pseudonym), or under the form of name mentioned in the title (**Bulwer** in one book, **Lytton** in another, **Bulwer Lytton** in a third; **Sherlock**, Th., in that divine's earlier works; **Bangor**, Th. [Sherlock], *Bp. of*, in later ones; **Salisbury**, Th. [Sherlock], *Bp. of*, in the next issues; **London**, Th. [Sherlock], *Bp. of*, in his last works; **Milnes**, R. Monckton, for "Good night and good morning" and the nine other works published before 1863, and **Houghton**, Rich. M. M., *Baron*, for the 1870 edition of "Good night and good morning" and for other books published since his ennoblement), or under the name of editor or translator when the author's name is not given, as proposed by Mr. Crestadoro. This might have been best with object A; but we have also object D to provide for, — the finding of all the books of a given author, — and this can most conveniently be done if they are all collected in one place.

A. Author.

1. Personal.

a. Under whom as author.

2. Enter works written conjointly by several authors under the name of the one first mentioned on the title-page, with references from the others.

Ex. **Schiller**, Joh. Christoph Fried. v., *and* **Humboldt**, K. W., *Freiherr* v. Briefwechsel. Stuttg., 1830. 16°.

Humboldt, Karl Wilhelm, *Freiherr* v. Briefwechsel. *See* **Schiller**, J. C. F. v., *and* **Humboldt**, K. W. v.

When countries are joint authors it is better to make full entries under each and arrange them as if the country under consideration were the only one. Each country puts its own name first in its own edition of a joint work; and the arrangement proposed avoids an additional complexity under countries, which are confusing enough at the best.

Whether the joint authorship appears in the title or not should make no difference in the mode of entry; if one name appears on the title, that should be chosen for the entry; if none, take the most important.

3. Distinguish between joint authors of one work and two authors of separate works joined in one volume. In the latter case, if there is no collective title, the heading should be the name of the first author alone and an analytical reference should be made from the second.

Ex. "The works of Shelley and Keats" would be entered in full under **Shelley** (both names being mentioned in the title but Shelley alone in the heading), and analytically (§ 93) under **Keats**. In such cases a double heading would often mislead.

4. Consider the respondent or defendant of a thesis as its author, except when it unequivocally appears to be the work of the præses.

5. Enter pseudonymous works under the author's real name, when it is known, with a reference from the pseudonym.

One is strongly tempted to deviate from this rule in the case of writers like George Eliot and George Sand, Gavarni and Grandville, who appear in literature only under their pseudonyms. It would apparently be much more convenient to enter their works under the name by which alone they are known and under which everybody but a professed cataloguer would assuredly look first. For an author-catalogue this might be the best plan, but in a dictionary catalogue, we have to deal with such people not merely as writers of books, but as subjects of biographies or parties in trials, and in such cases it seems proper to use their legal names. Besides, if one attempts to exempt a few noted writers from the rule given above, where is the line to be drawn? No definite principle of exception can be laid down which will guide either the cataloguer or the reader; and probably the confusion would in the end produce greater inconvenience than the present rule. Moreover, the entries made by using the pseudonym as a heading would often have to be altered. For a long time it would have been proper to enter the works of Dickens under **Boz**; the Dutch annual bibliography uniformly uses Boz-Dickens as a heading. No one would think of looking under **Boz** now. Mark Twain is in a transition state. The public mind is divided between Twain and Clemens. The tendency is always toward the use of the real name; and that tendency will be much helped in the reading public if the real name is always preferred in catalogues. Some pseudonyms persistently adopted by authors have come to be considered as the only names, as **Voltaire** (see §§ 14, 15), and the translation **Melanchthon** (see § 19). Perhaps George **Sand** and George **Eliot** will in time be adjudged to belong to the same company. It would be well if cataloguers could appoint some permanent committee with authority to decide this and similar points as from time to time they occur.

6. When the illustrations form a very important part of a work, consider both the author of the text and the designer — or in certain cases the engraver — of the plates to be author, and make a full entry under each. Under the author mention the designer's name in the title and vice versa.

Such works are: Walton's Welsh scenery, with text by Bonney; Wolf's "Wild animals," with text by Elliot. Which shall be taken as author in the subject- or form-entry depends upon the work and the subject. Under **Water-color drawings** it would be Walton; under **Wood-engravings**, Wolf; under **Wales** and **Zoölogy**, the cataloguer must decide which illustrates the subject most, the writer or the artist. *E. g.*, under **Gothic Architecture** Pugin is undoubtedly to be considered the author of his "Examples" though "the literary part" is by E. J. Willson; for the illustrator was really the author and the text was subsidiary to the plates. It was to carry out Pugin's ideas not Willson's that the work was published.

6½. The designer or painter copied is the author of engravings; the cartographer is the author of maps; the engraver in general is to be considered as no more the author than the printer. But in a special catalogue of engravings the engraver would be considered as author; in any full catalogue references should be made from the names of famous engravers as Raimondi, Müller, Steinla, Wolle.

7. Enter musical works doubly, under the author of the words and also the composer of the music.

Short and Medium will generally enter only under the composer; Don Giovanni, for example, only under **Mozart** and not under Da **Ponte**. This economy especially applies to songs.

8. Booksellers and auctioneers are to be considered as the authors of their catalogues, unless the contrary is expressly asserted.

Entering these only under the form-heading **Catalogues** belongs to the dark ages of cataloguing. Put the catalogue of a library under the library's name. (§ 40.)

9. Enter commentaries with the text complete under the author of the text and also under the author of the commentary, provided that is entitled "Commentary on * * *" and not "* * * with a commentary."

In a majority of cases this difference in the title will correspond to a difference in the character of the works and in the expectation of the public; if in any particular case the commentary preponderates in a title of the second of the forms above, a reference can be made from the commentator's name.

10. Enter a continuation or an index, when not written by the author of the original work but printed with it, under the same heading, with an analytical reference from its own author; when printed separately, enter it under each author. An epitome should be entered under the original author, with a reference from the epitomator.

11. Enter concordances both under their own author and the author concorded. The latter entry however is to be regarded as a subject-entry.

Ex. **Cleveland's** Concordance to the poetical works of **Milton, Brightwell's** Concordance to **Tennyson**, Mrs. **Furness's** Concordance to **Shakespeare's** poems.

12. Reporters are usually treated as authors of reports of trials, *etc.*[1] Translators and editors are not to be considered as authors.[2] (But see References, § 44.)

[1] A stenographic reporter is hardly more an author than the printer is; but it is not well to attempt to make fine distinctions.

[2] A collection of works should be entered under the translator if he is also the collector (see § 43); but again if he translates another man's collection it should be put under the name of the original collector; as Dasent's "Tales from the North" is really a version of part of **Asbjörnsen** *and* **Moe's** "Norske Folkeventyr" and belongs under their names as joint collectors, with a reference from **Dasent**.

b. Under what part of the name.

13. Put under the Christian or first name:

a. Sovereigns or princes of sovereign houses. Use the English form of the name.

The direction "Use the English form of the name" was a concession to ignorance; when it was given, that form was almost alone employed in English books; since then the tone of literature has changed; the desire for local coloring has led to the use of foreign forms and we have become familiarized with Louis, Henri, Marguerite, Carlos, Karl, Wilhelm, Gustaf. If the present tendency continues we shall be able to treat princes' names like any other foreign names; perhaps the next generation of cataloguers will no more tolerate the headings **William** *Emperor of Germany,* **Lewis** XIV than they will tolerate **Virgil, Horace, Pliny**. The change, to be sure, would give rise to some difficult questions of nationality, but it would diminish the number of the titles now accumulated under the more common royal names.

b. Persons canonized.

Ex. **Thomas** [a **Becket**], *Saint.*

c. Friars who by the constitution of their order, drop their surname. Add the name of the family in parentheses and refer from it.

Ex. **Paolino da S. Bartolomeo** [J. P. **Wesdin**].

d. Persons known under their first name only, whether or not they add that of their native place or profession or rank.

Ex. **Paulus** *Diaconus,* **Thomas** *Heisterbacensis.*

e. Oriental authors, including Jewish rabbis whose works were published before 1700.

Ex. **Abu Bekr ibn Bedr**. This rule has exceptions. Some Oriental writers are known and should be entered under other parts of their name than the first, as "**Abu-l-Kasim,** Khalaf ibn Abbas," or under some appellation as "al-**Masudi,**" "at-**Tabari**." Grässe's "Lehrbuch einer allgemeinen Literärgeschichte" is a convenient guide in this matter; he prints that part of the name by which Arabic writers are commonly known in a heavier type than the rest.

14. Put under the surname:

a. In general, all persons not included under § 13.

b. In particular, British noblemen and ecclesiastical dignitaries; all other noblemen under their highest titles. Refer.

Ex. **Stanhope**, Philip Dormer, *4th Earl of Chesterfield.* **Kaye**, John, *Bishop of Lincoln.* **Saint-Simon**, Louis de Rouvroi, *duc* de.

This is the British Museum rule and Mr. Jewett's; Mr. Perkins prefers entry under titles for British noblemen also, in which I should agree with him if the opposite practice were not so well established. The reasons for entry under the title are that British noblemen are always so spoken of, always sign by their titles only, and seldom put the family name upon the title-pages of their books, so that ninety-nine in a hundred readers must look under the title first. The reasons against it are that the founders of noble families are often as well known —sometimes even better—by their family name as by their titles (as Charles Jenkinson afterwards Lord Liverpool, Sir Robert Walpole afterwards Earl of Orford); that the same man bears different titles in different parts of his life (thus P. Stanhope published his "History of England from the peace of Utrecht" as Lord Mahon and his "Reign of Queen Anne" as Earl Stanhope); that it separates members of the same family (Lord Chancellor Eldon would be under **Eldon** and his father and all his brothers and sisters under the family name **Scott**), and brings together members of different families (thus the earldom of Bath has been held by members of the families of Shaunde, Bourchier, Granville, and Pulteney, and the family name of the present Marquis of Bath is Thymne), which last argument would be more to the point in planning a family history. The same objections apply to the entry of French noblemen under their titles, about which there can be no hesitation. The strongest argument in favor of the Museum rule is that it is well-established and that it is desirable that there should be some uniform rule. Ecclesiastical dignitaries stand on an entirely different footing. There is much more use of the family name and much more change of title.

c. Married women, using the surname of the last husband, or, if divorced, the name then resumed. Refer.

I should be inclined to make an exception in the case of those wives who continue writing, and are known in literature, only under their maiden names (as Miss **Freer** or Fanny **Lewald**), were we sure of dealing with them only as authors, but they may be subjects; we may have lives of them, for instance, which ought to be entered under their present names.

15. Put the works of authors who change their name under the latest form, provided the new name be legally and permanently adopted.

If the change consist in the addition of a name the new name is to be treated by the next rule.

16. Put compound names:

a. If English, under the last part of the name, when the first has not been used alone by the author.

This rule requires no investigation and secures uniformity; but like all rules, it sometimes leads to entries under headings where nobody would look for them. Refer.

b. If foreign, under the first part.

Both such compound names as **Gentil-Bernard** and such as **Gentil de Chavagnac.** There are various exceptions, as **Fénelon**, not **Salignac de Lamothe Fénelon, Voltaire,** not **Arouet de Voltaire.** Moreover it is not always easy to determine what is a compound surname in French. A convenient rule would be to follow the authority of Hœfer (Biog. gén.) and Quérard, in such cases, if they always agreed; unfortunately they often differ. References are necessary whichever way one decides each case.

17. Put surnames preceded by prefixes:

a. In French, under the prefix when it is or contains an article, **Le, La, L', Du, Des**; under the word following when the prefix is a preposition, **de, d'.**

b. In English, under the prefix, as **De Quincey, Van Buren,** with references when necessary.

c. In all other languages under the name following the prefix, as **Gama,** Vasco da, with references whenever the name has been commonly used in English with the prefix, as **Del Rio, Vandyck, Van Ess.**

Prefixes are d', de, de La (the name goes under *La* not *de*), Des, Du, L', La, Le, Les, St., Ste. (to be arranged as if written Saint, Sainte), Van, A', Ap, O', Fitz, Mac (which is to be printed as it is in the title, whether M', or Mc, or Mac, but to be arranged as if written Mac).

18. Put names of Latin authors under that part of the name chosen in

Smith's Dictionary of Greek and Roman biography, unless there is some good reason for not doing so.

19. Put names of capes, lakes, mountains, rivers, forts, *etc.*, beginning with Cape, Lake, Mt., etc., under the word following the prefix, but when the name is itself used as a prefix, do not transpose Cape, etc.

Ex. **Cod, Cape; George, Lake; Washington, Mt.; Moultrie, Fort;** but **Cape Breton Island.** When the name of a fort becomes the name of a city of course the inversion must be abandoned, as **Fort Wayne.**

c. Under what form of the name.

20. Give the names, both family and Christian, in the vernacular form,[1] if any instance occurs of the use of that form in the printed publications of the author.[2]

[1] The vernacular form of most Christian names may be found in Michaelis's "Wörterbuch der Taufnamen" (Berlin, 1856). There are also meagre lists in foreign dictionaries. (On the names of sovereigns, see § 13; on the Latin names of Greek authors, see § 25; on the names of Greek gods, see § 70.)

[2] This is the British Museum rule. It will obviously be sometimes impossible and often difficult to determine this point in a library of less extent than the Museum, and the cataloguer must make up his mind to some inconsistency in his treatment of mediæval names, and be consoled by the knowledge that if proper references are made no harm will be done. Against a too great preference of the vernacular Prof. De Morgan writes in the preface to his "Arithmetical books:" "I have not attempted to translate the names of those who wrote in Latin at a time when that language was the universal medium of communication. I consider that the Latin name is that which the author has left to posterity, and that the practice of retaining it is convenient, as marking, to a certain extent, the epoch of his writings, and as being the appellation by which his contemporaries and successors cite him. It is well to know that Copernicus, Dasypodius, Xylander, Regiomontanus, and Clavius were Zepernik, Rauchfuss, Holtzmann, Müller, and Schlüssel. But as the butchers' bills of these eminent men are all lost, and their writings only remain, it is best to designate them by the name they bear on the latter, rather than the former."

The same may be said of Camerarius (Kämmerer), Capito (Kopflein), Mercator (Kramer), Œcolampadius (Hausschein,) where it would be useless to employ the vernacular name; if both forms are in use, as in the case of Pomeranius=Bugenhagen, the vernacular should have the preference. Reuchlin is much more common than its equivalent, Capnio. — Before the Reformation the presumption is in favor of the Latin form; after it in favor of the vernacular.

21. When an author's name is variously spelled, select the best authorized form as heading, add the variants in parentheses, and make references from them to the form adopted.

Of course great care must be taken not to enter separately works in which an author spells his name differently, as Briant and Bryant, Easterbrookes and Estabrook, Erdmann and Erdtmann. On the other hand different people who spell their names differently should be separated, as Hofmann and Hoffmann, Maier, Mair, Majer, Mayer, Mayr, Meier, Meir, Mejer, Meyer, Meyr, Schmid, Schmidt, Schmied, Schmiedt, Schmit, Schmitt, Smith, Smyth, Smythe.

In German Christian names there is a want of uniformity in the use of C and K (Carl, Conrad, Karl, Konrad) and f and ph (Adolf, Adolph). Occasionally an author uses both forms in different books, or writing only in Latin (Carolus, Rudolphus) does not show which form he prefers. Where the author thus leaves the point undecided K and f should be preferred to C and ph.

22. Give name of places in the English form.

Munich not **Muenchen, Vienna** not **Wien.**

23. But if both the English and the foreign form are used by English writers prefer the foreign form.

24. Use the modern name of a city and refer to it from the ancient, provided their existence has been continuous and there is no doubt as to the identity.

25. In transliteration of names from alphabets of differently formed letters, use the vowels according to their German sounds.

I. e., **a** (not *ah*) for the sound of *a* in *father,* **e** (not *a*) for the sound of *e* in *heir* or of *a* in *hate,* **i** (not *e*) for the sound of *i* in *mien,* **u** (not *oo* nor *ou*) for the sound of *u* in *true* or of *oo* in *moon.* This practice makes transliterations that are likely to be pronounced in the main correctly by anyone who knows any language but his own (who would naturally give foreign vowel sounds to foreign names), and will give transliterations agreeing at least in part with those of other nations. In some points, however, we must be careful not to be misled by the practice of foreigners, and when we take a name from Russian, for instance, through the French or German, must see to it that the necessities of their alphabet have not led them to use letters that do not suit our system. A Frenchman writes for Turgenief *Tourguénef,* and for Golovin *Golovine.* A German for Dershavin writes *Derschawin,* and, worse than that, is obliged to use the clumsy *dsch* where an Englishman can use j, as *Dschellaleddin* for Jalal-ad-Din. (See the interesting preface and introduction of J. Thomas's Dict. of Biog., Phila., Lippincott, 1870, where, however, a very different orthography is recommended.)

In *Arabic* names I am advised by good scholars to uniformly write **a** where our ordinary Anglicized names have **e**, except for Ebn and Ben which become Ibn and Bin; also **i** for **ee**, and **u** where **o** has been commonly used; in other words to uniformly represent the vowel fatha by **a**, kasra by **i**, and dhamma by **u**. Thus **Mohammed** becomes **Muhammad**, **Abou ed-Deen** becomes **Abu ad-Din**. Of course references must be made from the corrupt forms under which various Arabic authors have become known in the West unless it is thought that the altered form has been so commonly used that it must be taken for the entry, as perhaps **Avicenna** from Ibn Sina, **Averroes** from Ibn Roshd.

In *Danish* names if the type **å** is not to be had, use its older equivalent **aa**; in a manuscript catalogue the modern orthography, **å**, should be employed. Whichever is chosen should be uniformly used, however the names may appear in the books. The diphthong **æ** should not be written **ae**, nor should **ö** be written **oe**; **ö**, not **œ**, should be used for **ø**.

In *Dutch* names write **y** for the modern **ij** and arrange so.

In *German* names used as headings, for **ä, ö, ü**, write **ae, oe, ue**, and arrange accordingly.

For *ancient Greek* names use the Latinized form, as **Democritus** not **Demokritos**, **Longinus** not **Logginos**. This holds good of translated works as well as of the originals. It will not do to enter an Italian version of the Odyssey under **Omero**, or of the Euterpe under **Erodoto**, or a French version of the Noctes Atticæ under **Aulu-Gelle**.

For *modern Greek* names Prof. Abbot proposes the following plan. Works in Romaic to be entered in a supplement, the names not transliterated but printed in the Greek type. Translations of works of modern Greek authors to be put under their Greek names in the supplement, with references in the main catalogue under the forms (whatever they may be) which their names assume in the translation. Original works written in French, German, English, etc., by modern Greek authors may be treated in the same way if their authors have not become French, German, or English by residence and literary labors, in which case they should be entered under the French, German, or English forms which they have chosen for their names, with cross references, if necessary, from the Greek supplement to these names. If, however, transliteration is attempted the following table of equivalents may be used:

αι	æ	η	i	β	v	κ after γ	g
αυ	av	ηυ	iv	γ	gh	ξ	x
ει	ei	οι	œ	γ before κ, γ, χ, ξ	n	ου	u
ευ	ev	υ	y			ρ	r
		υι	yi	δ	dh	χ	kh

In *Hungarian* names write **ö, ü,** with the diæresis (not **oe, ue**), and arrange like the English **o, u.**

In *Spanish* names use the modern orthography **i** and **j** rather than the ancient **y** and **x.**

In *Swedish* names **ä, å, ö,** should be so written (not **ae, oe**), and arranged as the English **a, o.**

Ballhorn's Grammatography (London, 1861) will be found very useful on such points.

2. Corporate.

General principle.

26. Bodies of men are to be considered as authors of works published in their name or by their authority.

The chief difficulty with regard to bodies of men is to determine (1) what their names are and (2) whether the name or some other word shall be the heading. In regard to (2) the catalogues hitherto published may be regarded as a series of experiments. No satisfactory usage has as yet been established. Local names have always very strong claims to be headings; but to enter the publications of all bodies of men under the places with which the bodies are connected would push a convenient practice so far that it becomes inconvenient and lead to many rules entirely out of harmony with the rest of the catalogue.

Details.

27. Enter under places (countries, or parts of countries, cities, towns, ecclesiastical, military, or judicial districts) the works published officially by their rulers (kings,[1] governors, mayors, prelates, generals commanding, courts,[2] etc.).

[1] Of course this does not affect works written privately by kings, etc., as K. James's "Counterblast."

[2] The relation of courts to judicial districts is a little different from the others, but it is convenient to treat them alike.

28. Similarly Congress, Parliament, and other governmental bodies are authors of their journals, acts, minutes, laws, etc.; and other departments of government of their reports, and of the works published by them or under their auspices.

These are to be entered under the name of the country, city, or town, and not in the main alphabet under the word **Congress, Parliament, City Council,** or the like.

29. Laws on one or more particular subjects whether digested or merely collected must have author-entries both under the name of the country and under the name of the collector or digester.

Ex. Tilsley's "Digest of the stamp acts" would appear both under **Great Britain** and **Tilsley.**

30. Works written officially are to be entered under the name of the department of government or ecclesiastical district or society (see § 40) with a reference from the name of the official if it is thought worth making.

Some libraries may refer always; most will refer only when the report has exceptional importance (1) from its subject, (2) from the treatment of its subject, (3) from its literary merits, (4) from the fame of its author, or (5) from having been separately published. Horace Mann's reports, for example, should be catalogued under **Massachusetts.** *Board of Education,* to which heading a reference should be made from **Mann.** President's messages should appear under **United States.** *President.* Proclamations and all other official writings of kings should appear under the name of the country (division *King* or *Crown*), arranged by reigns, as,

Great Britain. *King.*	**United States.** *President.*
Charles I.	*Buchanan.*
Charles II.	*Lincoln.*
James II.	*Johnson.*
William and Mary.	*Grant.*

31. "Articles to be inquired of" in ecclesiastical districts should go under the name of the district; but episcopal charges are not to go under the name of the bishopric unless they relate especially to its affairs, in which case they will have a subject-entry.

Ex. **York, Archdeaconry of.** Articles to be enquired of within the A. of Y.

32. Reports made to a department but not by an official are to be entered under the department with either an entry, reference, or analytical, under the author, as circumstances require.

Gould's "Mollusca and shells" and **Cassin's** "Mammalogy and ornithology of the United States Exploring Expedition under Wilkes" are of this nature; so is "Memorial ceremonies at the graves of our soldiers, collected under authority of Congress by Frank Moore."

33. Enter congresses of several nations under the name of the place of meeting (as that usually gives them their name), with references from the nations taking part in them and from any name by which they are popularly known.

Ex. The Congress of **London,** of **Paris,** of **Verona.**

34. Enter treaties under the name of each of the contracting parties, with a reference from the name of the place, when the treaty is commonly called by that name, and from any other usual appellation.

Ex. Treaty of **Versailles, Barrier** treaty, **Jay's** treaty.

35. Enter the official publications of any political party[1] or religious denomination or order,[2] or military order, under the name of the party, or denomination, or order.[3]

[1] Platforms, manifestoes, addresses, *etc.*, under **Democratic Party, Republican Party,** etc.

[2] Confessions of faith, creeds, catechisms, liturgies, breviaries, missals, hours, offices, prayer books, etc., under **Baptists, Benedictines, Catholic Church, Church of England,** etc.

[3] That part of a body which belongs to any place should be entered under the name of the body not the place; *e. g.*, **Congregationalists in New England, Congregationalists in Massachusetts,** not **New England Congregationalists, Massachusetts Congregationalists.** But references must be made from the place; (indeed in cases like Massachusetts Convention, Essex Conference, it may be doubted whether those well known names should not be the headings). It is to be noticed this rule is just the reverse of the one given under Subjects, § 68. Single churches have usually been entered under the place; a practice which arose in American catalogues from our way of naming churches "The First Church in ——," "The Second Church in ——," etc., and applies very well to a majority of English churches, whose name generally includes the name of the parish. It would be more in accordance with dictionary principles to limit the local entry of churches to 1st church, *etc.*, and those which have only the name of the town or parish, and to put all others (as **St. Sepulchre's, St. Mary Aldermansbury**) under their names, as they read, and to treat convents and monasteries in the same way. (But see § 40, Rule 2.) Of course the parishes of London (as Kensington, Marylebone, Southwark) like the parts of Boston (Dorchester, Roxbury, etc.), or of any other composite city, will be put under their own names, not under the name of the city.

36. Enter reports, journals, minutes, etc., of conventions, conferences, etc., under the names of the bodies holding the conferences, etc. When the body has no exact name[1] enter under the name of the place of meeting.[2]

[1] Some conventions are held by bodies which have no existence beyond the convention. If, however, they have a definite name use that; *ex.* 4th **National Quarantine and Sanitary Convention**. Often the name is given in different forms. Select that which appears to be the most authentic and make references from the others.

[2] In any case it is well to refer from the name of the place, and in the case of Presidential conventions it is indispensable.

Put the convention of a county or other named district under the name of the district, with a reference from the town in which it is held, when it is named in the title-page.

37. Enter ecclesiastical councils, both general and special, under the name of the place of meeting. (The Vatican Council under **Vatican** not **Rome.**) Refer from the name of the ecclesiastical body.

38. Enter reports of committees under the name of the body to which they belong; but reports of "a committee of citizens," *etc.*, not belonging to any named body should be put under the name of the writer, if known, if not, of the chairman, or if that is not given, of the first signer, or if not signed, under the name of the place.

39. Put the anonymous publications of any class (not organized) of citizens of a place under the place.

Ex. "Application to Parliament by the merchants of London," should go under **London. Merchants.**

40. Societies are authors of their journals, memoirs, proceedings, transactions, publications. (On publishing-societies, see B. Substitutes, § 43, *d.*)

The chief practices in regard to societies have been to enter them (1. British Museum) under a special heading—**Academies**—with a geographical arrangement; (2. Boston Public Library, printed catalogue) under the name of the place where they have their headquarters; (3. Harvard College Library and Bost. Pub. Lib., present system) under the name of the place, *if it enters into the legal name of the society,* otherwise under the first word of that name not an article; (4. Boston Athenæum) English societies under the first word of the society's name not an article, foreign societies under the name of the place. Both 3 and 4 put under the place all purely local societies, those whose membership or objects are confined to the place. The 1st does not deserve a moment's consideration; such a heading is out of place in an author-catalogue, and the geographical arrangement only serves to complicate matters and render it more difficult to find any particular academy. The 2d is utterly unsuited to American and English societies. The 3d practice is simple; but it is difficult to see the advantage of the exception which it makes to its general rule of entry under the society's name; the exception does not help the cataloguer, for it is just as hard to determine whether the place enters into the *legal* name as it is to ascertain the name; it does not help the reader, for he has no means of knowing whether the place is part of the legal name or not. The 4th is simple and intelligible; it is usually easy for both cataloguer and reader to determine whether a society is English or foreign. I shall mention two other possible plans, well aware that there are strong objections to both, but believing that plan 5 is on the whole the best.

5TH PLAN. *Rule* 1. Enter academies, associations, institutes, universities, societies, libraries, galleries, museums, colleges, and all similar bodies, both English and foreign, according to their corporate name, neglecting an initial article when there is one.

Exception 1. Enter the royal academies of Berlin, Göttingen, Leipzig, Lisbon, Madrid,

Munich, St. Petersburg, Vienna, etc., and the "Institut" of Paris, under those cities. An exception is an evil; this one is adopted because the academies are almost universally known by the name of the cities, and are hardly ever referred to by the name Königliches, Real, etc.

Exception 2. Enter London guilds under the name of the trade; *e. g.*, "**Stationers' Company,**" not "Master and Keepers or Wardens and Commonalty of the Mystery and Art of Stationers of the City of London," which is the corporate title. This exception is adopted because (1) it gives a heading easier to find and (2) it would be difficult in many cases to ascertain the real names of the London companies.

Exception 3. Enter American state historical societies under the name of the state.

Rule 2. Enter churches and all local benevolent or moral or similar societies under the name of the place. Young men's Christian associations, Mercantile library associations, and the like are to be considered local. Business firms or corporations, libraries, galleries, museums, are not to be considered local, nor are private schools local, but go under their corporate name, or, if they are not corporate, under the name of the proprietor. Public schools and libraries and galleries instituted or supported by a city go under the name of the city. If college societies are considered local they would be entered not under the name of the place but of the college; if they are treated by Rule 1, reference (6) must be made.

Refer (1) from all the varying forms of the society's name.
(2) from important words in the society's name, when the first word is unlikely to be thought of.
(3) from the name of the city where the society is situated.
(4) from the motto in the names of Dutch societies.
(5) from the names of the royal societies of Berlin, &c.
(6) from colleges to college societies.
(7) from such words as **Gallery, Museum,** etc., to all the galleries, museums, etc., contained in the catalogue.

The plan might be tabulated thus

Under name.	*Under place.*
Societies not local.	Local societies.
English and American academies.	Academies of the European Continent and of South America.
Colleges, libraries, galleries, museums not municipal.	Municipal colleges, libraries, galleries.
Private schools.	Public schools.
Business firms and corporations.	Municipal corporations.
London guilds (name of trade).	State historical societies (name of state).

Buildings are for the most part provided for in the above rules as museums, galleries, libraries, churches, etc. Any others should be entered under their names with a reference from the city.

The 6TH PLAN has the same rules as the first and *no* exceptions. It may be preferred by those who think the advantage of having a single uniform rule greater than the inconvenience of unusual headings.

B. SUBSTITUTES.

Substitutes for the author's name (to be chosen in the following order) are:

41. Part of the author's name when only a part is known.

Ex. For a book "by J. B. Far - - -," or "by L. M. P.," the entry is to be made under **Far** - - -, J. B., **P.**, L. M. If the last initials are evidently, from the style of printing, those of a title, the entry will be under the initial preceding them; thus for books "by B. F., *D.D.*," or "by M. P. R., *Gent.*," or "by X. Y. Z., *D.D.*," the entry is to be made under **F.**, B., *D.D.*, and **R.**, M. P., *Gent.*, and **Z.**, X. Y., *D.D.* In such case it is safest to have also a reference from the last initial to the one chosen, as **D.**, X. Y. Z. D. *See* **Z.**, X. Y., *D.D.* It is often well to make a reference from the first word (title-reference).

42. A pseudonym, that is, a false name, as John **Phenix**, Mark **Twain.**

If the author's real name is known make the entry under that with a reference from the pseudonym.

A phrase—"One who loves his country," "A friend to peace"—or even a shorter appellation —"A lawyer"— is not a name. References might be made from these to the word under which the book is entered, but they would swell the catalogue and rarely be of use. Latin phrases, like "Amator patriæ," should be treated as names and the entry made under the last word, as **Patriæ**, Amator. But it should not be made under patronymic adjectives, or certain words like junior, senior, evidently intended to qualify the name, not to be taken as the name; *i. e.,* the heading for a book "by Phileleutherus Lipsiensis" would not be **Lipsiensis**, Phileleutherus, but **Phileleutherus** *Lipsiensis;* Vanity Fair album by Jehu Junior would go under **Jehu** *junior,* not **Junior**, Jehu. In such cases a reference from the word which is not taken as the heading will be an additional safeguard.

The word Anonymus may be considered as a pseudonym when used as follows, "Anonymi introductio in," etc.

43. Collector.

That is, the one who is responsible for the existence of a collection. A collection is made by putting together, with a collective title, three or more works by different authors so as to make one work. *Examples:* Rossiter's "Little classics," Buchon's "Collection des mémoires."

a. This rule does not apply to the collector (editor) of a periodical.

b. Several works published together without a collective title are to be put under that author's-name which appears first on the title-page, even though the collector's name is also there; in other words he is then to be considered merely as the editor.

Thus "The fraternitye of vacabondes, by J. Awdeley; A caueat for commen cursetors, by T. Harman; A sermon in praise of thieves, by Parson Haben or Hyberdyne; those parts of The groundworke of conny-catching that differ from Harman's Caueat; ed. by E. Viles and F. J. Furnivall," should be entered not under **Viles**, E., *and* **Furnivall**, F. J., but under **Awdeley**; but if it had been entitled "Early tracts on vagabonds and beggars; edited by E. Viles and F. J. Furnivall," it would properly be put under the editors.

c. If the collector's name is known the collection is to be put under it, whether it occurs on the title-page or not. If his name is not known enter the collection like any anonymous work, under the first word of the collective title. In either case the separate works forming the collection must be entered under their respective authors. (See V. Analysis.) Title-references are also often necessary. (See III. Titles.)

d. Societies like the Camden, Chetham, Hakluyt are collectors of the series of works published by them, of which a list should be given under their names.

But every such work filling one or more volumes should be entered separately under its author or title as if it were published independently, and should have the same subject-entry. (See § 91.) Works that fill part of a volume are to be entered analytically. (See § 92.) Of course any volume consisting of three or more treatises, put together with a collective title by the society, should be entered under it as collector, if no collector's name is given.

For anonymous works, see Title-entry, § 53. For trials, see § 48.

C. References.

44. Make references

(2.) From joint authors (after the first) to the first.

(4.) From the præses to the respondent or defendant of a thesis or vice versâ.

(5.) From pseudonyms, initials, and part of names.

(6.) From important illustrators when not important enough for an entry.

(9.) From commentators who are not entitled to an entry, if the commentary preponderates or for any reason is likely to be looked for under the commentator's name. Where the line of omission shall be drawn depends on the fullness of the catalogue.

(10.) From the authors of continuations, indexes, and of introductions of some length.

(12.) From the names of reporters, translators, and editors of anonymous works and of works not anonymous which are commonly known by the name of their editors or translators.

Ex. Some translations from the German by **Mrs. Wister** are wrongly lettered, as if she were the author, and are therefore asked for by her name.

(13 *a.*) From the foreign form of names of sovereigns, whenever they are likely to be looked for under that form.

(13 *b, c.*) From the family name of persons canonized, and of friars who drop the family name on entering their order.

(13 *e.*) From such parts of Oriental names as require it.

(14 *b.*) From the titles of British noblemen to the family name, or vice versâ if the entry is made under the title.

From the family names of foreign noblemen, when they are known by them wholly or in part.

From the names of English sees and deaneries.

From any other title by which a man may be better known than by his real name.

As "**Claimant, The.**" The Diary of the Shah of Persia, catalogued under **Nassr-ad-Din,** requires a reference from **Shah.**

(14 *c.*) From the maiden names or first married names of wives to the last, provided they have written under the earlier names or for any other reason are likely to be looked for under them.

(15.) From the earlier forms of names that are changed.

(16.) From the first part of English compound names and the last part of foreign ones, whenever it seems necessary.

(17.) From the prefixes of foreign names when they have been commonly used in combination with the last part.

Ex. From **Vandyck** to **Dyck,** A. van, from **Degerando** to **Gerando,** and **De Candolle** to **Candolle.**

(18.) From the alternative part of Latin names.

(19–25.) From all forms of a name varying either by spelling, translation, or transliteration that do not come into immediate juxtaposition with the one chosen.

(30, 32.) From the authors of official writings (with discretion).

(33.) From nations taking part in a congress to the place of meeting.

(36.) From the places where conventions are held to the names of the bodies holding them.

(37.) From the name of an ecclesiastical body to the headings under which the councils of the body are entered.

(40.) A list of references is given in the note.

(41.) From part of the author's name appearing on the title-page to the whole name if discovered.

From the last initial given on a title-page to the one chosen for the entry.

(42.) From a pseudonym to the real name when discovered.

From some phraseological pseudonyms, especially if brief.

Ex. From **Lawyer** when an anonymous work is said to be "by a lawyer." For Full only.

From editors and translators.

If it is thought worth while to give a complete view of the literary and artistic activity of every author so far as it is represented in the library, of course references from editors, translators, illustrators, cartographers, engravers, *etc.*, must be made. But this completeness is not usually sought even in large libraries. Such references are also undeniably a help in finding books. But they increase the bulk and the cost of a catalogue so much, and are comparatively of so little use, that ordinary libraries must content themselves with a selection, though the best-made selection is certain to occasion complaints that the really useful ones have been omitted and the least important made. The chief classes of necessary references of this sort are:

(1.) From the editors of periodicals to the title-entry, when the periodical is commonly called by the editor's name, as Poggendorff's Annalen, Silliman's Journal.

(2.) From the names of editors and translators which are habitually mentioned in connection with a work, so that it is as likely to be looked for under the editor's as under the author's name. When the form is a combination of author's and editor's name, as Heyne's Virgil, Leverett's Cicero, the reference, though convenient, is certainly not necessary, inasmuch as a person of ordinary intelligence could hardly fail, not finding what he wanted under one name, to try the other.

(3.) From the names of those who have made poetical versions, on the ground that their work is something more than mere translation.

It may be thought that an excessive number of references is recommended, but it is plain that wherever there can be a reasonable doubt among cataloguers under what head a book ought to be entered, it should have at least a reference under each head. The object of an author-catalogue is to enable one to find the book; if that object is not attained the book might as well not be catalogued at all.

45. Make explanatory notes under such words as **Congress, Parliament, Academies, Societies,** and others in regard to whose entry there is a diverse usage, stating what is the rule of the catalogue.

D. Economies.

46. In the title-a-liners references are not an economy; they occupy as much room as an entry, and therefore the imprint may as well be given whenever the reference does not take the place of several titles.

47. Mr. Perkins would catalogue directories, state registers, and local gazetteers under the name of the place, omitting the author-entry. This is for Short alone, and should never be done by Full or Medium.

48. Trials may be entered only under the name of the defendant in a criminal suit and the plaintiff in a civil suit, and trials relating to vessels under the name of the vessel (subject-entries of course). But

Full and perhaps Medium should make author-entries under the reporter. It may be doubted, however, whether a stenographic reporter is entitled to be considered an author, any more than a type-setter.

49. Often in analysis it may be worth while to make a subject-entry and not an author-entry.

50. An economical device in some favor is to omit the entry under the author's name when the library contains only one work by him; so that many famous authors of whom no small library is likely to contain more than one work (such as Boswell, Dante, Gibbon, Lamb, Macaulay, Milton, indeed almost any of the English poets) will not appear in the catalogue; while the man who has written both a First class reader and a Second class reader, or a Mental arithmetic and a Written arithmetic, or two Sunday-school books, must be included. It is not necessary to say more to show the absurdity of the rule. If some authors must be omitted let it be those who the librarian knows are never called for, whether they have written one or fifty works.

51. Another objectionable economy is to put biographies under the name of the subject alone, omitting author-entry, so that there is no means of ascertaining whether the library possesses all the works of a given author.

II. TITLE-ENTRY.

First-word entry. (Anonymous works, 52, 53; Periodicals, 54; Fiction, 55; What is a first word, 56–58.)
First-word reference. (Plays and poems, 59; other works, 60.)
Catch-word reference. (Anonymous works, 61 *a*; other works, 61 *b*.)
Subject-word entry. (Anonymous biographies, 62.)
Subject-word reference. (Anonymous works, 63 *a*; other works, 63 *b*.)
Title-references to corporate entries, 64.
Double title-pages, 65.

TITLE-ENTRY.

52. Make a first-word entry for all[1] anonymous works,[2] except anonymous biographies, which are to be entered under the name of the subject of the life.[3] (If the author's náme can be ascertained insert it within brackets.)

[1]Of course there are exceptions to this rule. There are works which are always known by certain names, under which they should be entered although the title-pages of different editions may not begin with this name, or may not even contain it. The most noteworthy example is **Bible**, which is the best heading—in an English catalogue—for the Bible and for any of its parts in whatever language written and under whatever title published.

In cataloguing the anonymous books of the Middle Ages, "Incipit" or "Here begyns," or "Book the first of," and similar phrases are not to be considered as first words. Thus the history of the Seven Sages appears under the following variety of title:

1. Incipit historia septem sapientū Rome. [Cir. 1475.]
2. In hoc opusculo sunt subtilitates septē sapientū rome valde perutiles. [Later.]
3. Historia septem sapientum Romæ. 1490.
4. Historia calumnie nouercalis que septem sapientū inscribitur. 1490.
5. Ludus septem sapientum. [Cir. 1560.]

And the title of the versions are equally various:

1. Li romans des sept sages.
2. Li romans de Dolopathos.
3. Les sept sages de Rōme.
4. Les sept saiges de romme.
5. Los siete sabios de Roma.
6. Hienach volget ein gar schöne Cronick vñ hystori auss denn Geschichten der Römern.
7. Die hystorie uan die seuen wise mannen van Romen.
8. Hystory of the seuen maysters of Rome.
9. The Hystorie of the seven wise maisters of Rome.
10. The sevin seages.
11. De siu sive mestere.

Of course it will not do to catalogue these severally under Incipit, Hoc, Historia, Ludus, Romans, Sept, Siete, Hienach, Hystorie, Hystory, Sevin, and Siu. In this and other prose and poetical romances of the Middle Ages the heading must be taken in general from the subject of the romance; the name appearing of course in the original language, with all necessary references from other forms. In the present case all the editions would be collected under **Septem** sapientes,* with references from Ludus, Sept sages, Siete sabios, Hienach, and Seven, provided the library has so many editions.

Somewhat similarly collections of papers known by the name of a principal contributor or a

* Since this was in type I have come to the conclusion that all these should be entered under **Sandabad** (Lat. **Syntipas**), the reputed author of the original Indian romance. But the example will still serve to show the great variety in mediæval titles, and the inconvenience of following a strict first-word rule.

previous owner or of the house where they were found, should be entered under such name, or, if they must be entered under the name of an editor, should have a reference from such name; *ex.* Dudley papers, Winthrop papers, etc.

[2] A catalogue of authors alone finds the entry of its anonymous books a source of incongruity. The dictionary catalogue has no such trouble. It does not attempt to enter them in the author-catalogue until the author's name is known.

[3] For a smaller catalogue this may read "except anonymous works relating to a person, city, or other subject distinctly mentioned in the title, which are to be put under the name of the person, city, or subject." In the catalogue of a larger library where more exactness ("red-tape," "pedantry") is indispensable, biography should be the only exception, the place of entry under subjects and under large cities being too doubtful. And in planning a manuscript catalogue, it should be remembered that a small library may grow into a large one, and that if the catalogue is made in the best way at first there will be no need of alteration.

If a book's title-page is lost, and it is impossible to ascertain what it was, use the half-title or the running title, stating the fact; if it has neither, manufacture a title, within brackets.

53. Translations of anonymous works should be entered under the same heading as the original, whether the library possesses the original or not.

Ex. **Gisli's** saga. Story of Gisli the outlaw, from the Icelandic, by G. W. Dasent.

So Perron's translation, called by him "Glaive des couronnes," would appear under **Saif**-al-Tidjan; and the Arabian night's entertainments under **Alif** Laila. Criticisms of anonymous works must be put under the heading of the work criticised.

54. Periodicals are to be treated as anonymous and entered under the first word.

Ex. **Popular** science monthly, **Littell's** living age.

When a periodical changes its title the whole may be catalogued under the original title, with an explanatory note there and a reference from the new title to the old; or each part may be catalogued under its own title, with references, "For a continuation, *see* ," "For the previous volumes, *see* ."

Treat almanacs and other annuals as periodicals. Do not confound periodicals with serials. The four characteristics of a periodical are: (1) that it be published at intervals usually but not necessarily regular; (2) in general that the publication be intended to continue indefinitely; (3) that it be written by a number of contributors under the supervision of one or more editors; (4) that it consist of articles on various subjects, so that a set of the work does not form an organic whole. The 2d, 3d, and 4th criteria exclude works like Trollope's "The way we live now," and the "Encyclopædia Britannica." There are some exceptions to the 3d, as "Brownson's quarterly review."

Make a reference from the name of the editor when the periodical is commonly called by his name, as in the case of **Silliman's** Journal of science.

The Memoirs, Proceedings, Transactions of a society are periodicals in point of (1) occasional publication, (2) indefinite continuance, and—so far as they contain anything beyond the record of the society's meetings—of (4) variety of subject; but they lack the 3d characteristic, variety of authorship, inasmuch as the memoirs or other papers given in addition to "proceedings" proper may be considered as the work of the society acting through its members; the society, therefore, is the author and the Transactions, etc., need not have title-entry. There are, however, some "Journals" published by or "under the auspices of" societies which are really periodicals, and should be so treated in entry, the society being not the author but the editor. Again, there are works which occupy a borderland between the two classes, in regard to which the puzzled cataloguer should remember that it is not of much importance which way he decides, provided he is careful to make all necessary references. Examples of such doubtful cases are "Alpine journal: a record of mountain adventure and scientific observation. By members of the Alpine Club;" which contains nothing of or about the Club itself;—"Journal of the American Institute, a monthly publication devoted to the interests of agriculture, commerce, etc. Edited by a committee, members of the Institute," and "Journal of The Society of Arts and of The Institutions in Union," both of which are journals both in the sense of record of proceedings and of periodical publication.

55. Make a first-word entry for all works of prose fiction. (Include the author's name.)

Ex. **Daughter** of Heth; novel, by W. Black. London, 1874. 3 v. 8°.

If a proper name enters into the title the entry should be made under that; *ex.* **David** Copperfield, Life and adventures of, by C. Dickens.

56. When a title begins with an article the heading of a first-word entry or reference is the word following the article.

Ex. **Centaur,** The, not fabulous, *not* **The** centaur not fabulous. The entry has commonly been made under the first word "not an article or preposition." But it is found to work badly to except the preposition in the titles of novels and plays, and it is awkward to omit or transpose it in any case. One reason for excepting the article—that there would be an immense accumulation of titles under the unimportant words A, The, Le, Der, Uno, etc.—is not so strong in the case of prepositions; the other—that it is difficult to remember with what article a given title begins—hardly applies at all to prepositions. The preposition is full as likely to fasten itself in the memory as the word that follows it. The strongest argument in favor of confining preposition-entry to fiction and the drama is that in other cases the word following the preposition will probably be a subject-word, so that one entry will do the work of two. This will occasionally be true, but not often enough, I think, to make much difference.

57. When a title begins with a word expressive of the number which the work holds in a series the first-word entry or reference is to be made under the next word.

Ex. **Collection** of papers, 8th, *not* **Eighth** collection. **Letter**, 1st and 2d, to the Ministry, *not* **First** letter, etc., under **F**, and **Second** letter under **S**. Similarly Evening, Morning, Daily, and Weekly should be disregarded in titles of newspapers, otherwise we should have the morning edition at one end of the catalogue and the evening at the other. So "Appendix to," "Continuation of" are to be disregarded when they are followed by the title of the work continued.

58. When the first-word of a title is spelled unusually all the editions should be entered under the word spelled in the modern or correct way, with a reference from the form adopted in the title.

59. Make a first-word reference to the author for all plays, and for poems of some length or importance or notoriety.

Ex. **All's** well that ends well. *See* **Shakespeare,** W.
Nothing to wear. *See* **Butler,** W. A.

Of course entries are better than references for the reader; the latter are recommended here merely for economy, which will be found to be considerable when there are many editions of a play. It is much better to distribute these like any other title-references, through the alphabet than, as some have done, to collect the titles of novels together in one place and of plays in another. A man not unfrequently wishes to find a book whose title he has heard of without learning whether it was a novel, a play, a poem, or a book of travels.

If the catch-word of the title of a novel, poem, or play is the name of a real person who is its subject it is optional to make a reference as in § 56, or a biographical entry under the family name, or both.

Ex. **Paul** Revere's ride. *See* **Longfellow,** H. W.
or **Revere,** Paul. LONGFELLOW, H. W. (*In his* Tales of a way-side inn.)

60. Make a first-word reference to the author for other works which are likely to be inquired for under the first word of the title, whether because the title does not indicate the subject,[1] or because it is of a striking form,[2] or because the book is commonly known by its title,[3] or for any other good reason.

Ex. [1] Cuppé's "Heaven open to all men" needs a *title* reference, because for its *subject* it would be put under **Universal salvation** or **Future punishment, Duration of.** Hutton's "Plays and players" is merely an account of the New York stage. Keary's "Nations around" does not suggest any subject at all. [2] Border and bastille. [3] Divina commedia.

In a majority of cases, when a subject-word entry is made, no first-word reference is needed; but, if the title is striking, there should be a first-word reference, or a reference from that part of the title which is striking. Title-references should not generally be made from certain common titles, as "**Sermons** on various subjects," "**Essays,** historical and literary," and should be made from less common collective words, as "**Century** of painters," "**Century** of praise," etc. References should be liberally made to the works of such authors as Brown, Jones, Schmidt, Smith, Wilson; if one has forgotten the Christian name it is a work of too much time to find the book under the author, and one looks at once for a subject- or a title-entry or reference. And a reference will facilitate the finding of many collections entered properly under the editor; for it is easy to forget an editor's name, and often difficult to determine the subject-entry of a collection.

To sum up, then, make a title-reference when the author's name is common, the title memorable, or the subject obscure.

61. Make a catch-word reference or references

a. For all anonymous works which admit of it, if their subject does not appear distinctly from the title. To be made to the author if known, otherwise to the first word.

Ex. **Scarlet** gowns, True and exact account of the. *See* **True.** Here **Cardinals** is the subject, but the word does not occur in the title; **True** is the first-word and is therefore taken for the heading; but **Scarlet** gowns is a phrase very likely to remain in the memory of any-one who had seen the title, and therefore the reference is made. Books published under a comparatively unknown pseudonym should have either a first-word or a catch-word reference, unless their subject-entry can be easily inferred from the title.

b. For other works which are likely to be inquired for not under the first word but under the catch-word of the title. To be made to the author.

It is not easy to decide when to make such entries nor how many to make. "An account of the baronial mansions of England in the olden time" may be asked for as "Baronial halls" or as "English baronial halls" or perhaps as "Mansions of the olden time." If references are made from all possible headings which might occur to an inaccurate memory, there will be no end to the catalogue.

62. Make a subject-word entry for all anonymous biographies and works of a biographical character. (See § 52, note 3.)

Ex. **Cromwell,** Oliver. PERFECT politician, The; life of Cromwell. London, 1681. 8°.
— TREASON'S masterpiece; or, Conference between Oliver and a committee of Parliament. London, 1680. 8°.

For greater security this latter ought to have also a first-word reference.

63. Make a subject-word reference:

a. For all anonymous works which admit of it, to the author, if known, otherwise to the first word.

When the subject-word is the same as the heading of the subject-entry this reference need not be made; but it will not do to omit an important title-entry when there are many titles under the subject-heading or they are much subdivided, so that it would be difficult to find the title-entry there. Thus an anonymous book "France and the Pope" would no doubt have a subject-entry under some subdivision of **France**, but as this in a large catalogue would be little help towards finding the book, it should also have a reference among the titles which follow the subject **France**. Of course if there were only a dozen titles under France one entry would be enough.

b. For other works, when the subject-word is not the same as the name of the subject selected by the cataloguer.

In this case, however, a cross-reference, which will answer for all titles, is to be preferred to a collection of subject-word references, being more economical and nearly as convenient to the inquirer. Suppose, for instance, that **Insects** is preferred as a subject-name to **Entomology**. It will be better and more sparing of space to say once for all "**Entomology**. *See* **Insects**," referring a man to a part of the catalogue where he will find not only the book he seeks but many similar ones, than to make a number of references like these:

Entomologie, Cours de. *See* **Latreille**, P. A.
Entomologique, Bibliographie. *See* **Percheron**, A.
Entomology, Dialogues on. *See* **Dialogues**.
Entomology, Elements of. *See* **Dallas**, W. S.; **Ruschenberger**, W. S. W.
Entomology, Introduction to. *See* **Duncan**, J.; **Kirby**, W.

which will serve his turn only for the particular book he has in mind, and serve it very little better than the general reference.

64. Make title references (first-word, catch-word, or subject-word) for works which are entered under the names of societies or of governments.

The reason for this is that the inquirer might not think of looking for such works under those headings or might be unable to find them in the mass of titles under the larger countries, France, Great Britain, United States. But in view of the room which such references would fill, if made from all governmental titles, it seems best to state the rule for the entry of governmental and society publications very distinctly in the preface and then to require and presuppose a certain acquaintance with the plan of the catalogue on the part of those who use it, and omit all reference for ordinary official reports, making them only for works which have become part of literature, and are likely to be much inquired for; as the "Astronomical exploring expedition," "Connaissance des temps," "Description de l'Égypte," "Documents inédits," "Philosophical transactions," etc. Of course absolute uniformity cannot be secured in this way, but absolute uniformity is not very important. Even if occasionally a reference of this kind fails to be made which might reasonably be required, those which are made will be useful. It is easy to add the reference wanted in a manuscript catalogue, or in the inevitable supplement of a printed catalogue.

65. If a book has several title-pages use the most general, giving the others, if necessary, in a note or as contents.

This occurs especially in German books. The rule above should be followed even when the library has only one of the parts. But under the subject-heading the subtitle which corresponds to that subject may be used, the general title being given in a parenthesis after the imprint, so as to preserve the connection of the subject- and title-entries. *Ex.* VEHSE, E. Geschichte der Höfe des Hauses Sachsen. Hamburg, 1854. 7 v. 8°. (Vol. 28–34 *of his* Gesch. d. deut. Höfe.)

Title-references must sometimes be made from subtitles.

III. SUBJECTS.

A. Entries considered separately.

1. Choice between different subjects.

Between general and specific, 66; Between person and country, 67; Between subject and country, 68; Between subjects that overlap, 69.

2. Choice between different names.

Language, 70; Synonyms, 71–73; Subject-word and subject, 74; Homonyms, 75; Compound headings, 76; Double entry, 77–79; Vessels, 80; Civil actions, 81; Reviews, comments, etc., 82.

B. Entries considered as parts of a whole.

Cross-references, 85, 86; Synoptical table, 87.

SUBJECTS.

A. Entries considered separately.

Some questions in regard to the place of entry are common to the author- and the subject-catalogue; because individuals (persons, places, ships, etc.) may be at once authors and subjects. For these questions consult Part I, and also § 70 of the present part.

In a dictionary catalogue some books cannot profitably have subject-entry, because they not only have no one subject but do not even belong to any class of subjects.

A collection is to be entered under the word which expresses its subject or its general tendency. The memoirs, transactions, proceedings, etc., of a society should be entered under the name of the object for which the society is founded. When there are many societies under one head it is economical to refer merely; as from **Agriculture** or **Agricultural societies** to the various names.

The importance of deciding aright where any given subject shall be entered is in inverse proportion to the difficulty of decision. If there is no obvious principle to guide the cataloguer, it is plain there will be no reason why the public should expect to find the entry under one heading rather than another, and therefore in regard to the public it matters not which is chosen. But it is better that such decisions should be made to conform when possible to some general system, as there is then more likelihood that they will be decided alike by different cataloguers, and that a usage will grow up which the public will finally learn and profit by; as a usage has grown up in regard to the author-entry of French names containing De, Du, La, etc.

1. Choice between different subjects.

a. Between general and specific.

66. Enter a work under its subject-heading, not under the heading of a class which includes that subject.

Ex. Put Lady Cust's book on "The cat" under **Cat**, not under **Zoölogy** or **Mammals** or **Domestic animals**; and put Garnier's "Le fer" under **Iron**, not under **Metals** or **Metallurgy**.

This rule of "specific entry" is the main distinction between the dictionary catalogue and the alphabetico-classed.

Some subjects have no name; they are spoken of only by a phrase or by several phrases not definite enough to be used as a heading. A book may be written on the movements of fluids in plants, a very definite object of investigation, but as yet nameless; it must be put under Botany (Physiological). But if several works were written on it and it was called, let us say, **Phythydraulics**, it would be seen that, under this rule, it no more ought to be under **Botany** than **Circulation of the blood** under **Zoölogy**. Thirty years ago, "Fertilization of flowers" could hardly have been used as a heading; but late writings have raised it to the status of a subject. There are thousands of possible matters of investigation, some of which are from time to time discussed, but before the catalogue can profitably follow its "specific" rule in regard to them they must attain a certain individuality as objects of inquiry, and be given some sort of *name*, otherwise we must assign them class-entry.

And it is not always easy to decide what is a distinct subject. Many catalogues have a heading **Preaching**. Is Extempore preaching a sufficiently distinct matter to have a heading of its own? There are a number of books on this branch of the subject. In this particular case the difficulty can be avoided by making the heading **"Preaching without notes."** Many such questions may be similarly solved, with perhaps more satisfaction to the maker of the catalogue than to its users; but many questions will remain.

Then, mixed with this, and sometimes hardly distinguishable from it, is the case of subjects whose names begin with an unimportant adjective or noun,—Arc of the meridian, Capture of property at sea, Segment of a circle, Quadrature of the circle. All that can be said in such cases is that, if the subject be commonly recognized and the name accepted or likely to be accepted by usage, the entry must be made under it. For the fuller discussion of compound headings, see § 76.

On the other hand difficulty arises from the public, or a part of it, being accustomed to think of certain subjects in connection with their including classes, which especially happens to those persons who have used classed catalogues or the dictionary catalogues in which specification is only partially carried out; so that there is a temptation to enter certain books doubly, once under the specific heading to satisfy the rule, and once under the class to satisfy the public. The dictionary principle does not forbid this. If room can be spared the cataloguer may put what he pleases under an extensive subject (a class) provided he puts the less comprehensive works also under their respective specific headings. The objection to this is that, if all the specifics are thus entered, the bulk of the catalogue is enormously increased; and that, if a selection is made, it must depend entirely upon the "judgment," *i. e.*, the prepossessions and accidental associations of the cataloguer, and there will be an end to all uniformity, and probably the public will not be better satisfied, not understanding why they do not find class-entry in all cases.

b. Choice between person and country.

67. Put under the name of a king or other ruler all his biographies, and works purporting to be histories of his reign; but enter under the country all histories which include more than his reign and accounts of events which happened during the reign, and all political pamphlets not directly criticising his conduct.

The first part of this rule is analogous to that by which the works of a king of a private nature are put under his name, and all his public writings under the country; putting histories of the reign under the king is partly subject and partly title-entry. Books of this sort have really two subjects and ought to be entered twice (*e g.*, Boutaric's "La France sous Philippe le bel"); the rule above is simply an economical device to save room at the expense of convenience. Perhaps a better practice would be to enter all lives of kings as well as histories of their reigns under the country only, with a reference from the king.

Similarly there are some biographies and autobiographies which have such a very large proportion of history that they ought to appear both under the man and the country. In general we merely refer from the country, but occasionally nothing but double entry will suffice. Whether they shall appear by way of entry or merely be mentioned in a note, must be determined by circumstances.

c. Choice between event and country.

67½. Events[1] or periods[2] in the history of a country which have a proper name may be entered under that name with a reference from the

country; those whose name is common to many countries[3] should be entered under the country.

[1] St. Bartholomew's day. [2] Fronde. [3] Revolution; Restoration; Civil war.

d. Choice between subject (or form) and country.

The only satisfactory method is double entry under the local and the scientific subject,—to put, for instance, a work on the geology of California under both **California** and **Geology**, and to carry out this practice through the catalogue, so that the geographical student shall not be obliged to search for works on California under **Botany, Geology, Natural history, Palæontology, Zoölogy,** and a dozen similar headings, and the scientist shall not be sent to **California, England, Russia,** and a score of other places to find the various treatises on geology. But as this profusion of entry would make the catalogue very long, we are generally obliged to choose between country and scientific subject.

68. A work treating of a general subject with special reference to a place is to be entered under the place, with merely a reference from the subject.

Ex. Put Flagg's "Birds and seasons of New England" under **New England**, and under **Ornithology** say *See also* **New England.** As **New England ornithology** and **Ornithology of New England** are merely different names of the same specific subject it may be asked why we prefer the first. Because entry under **Ornithology of New England,** though by itself specific entry is, when taken in connection with the entries that would be grouped around it (**Ornithology, Ornithology of America, Ornithology of Scotland,** etc.) in effect class-entry; whereas the similar grouping under New England does not make that a class, inasmuch as **New England botany, New England history, New England ornithology** are not parts of New England but simply the individual New England considered in various aspects. Of course the dictionary catalogue in choosing between a class and an individual prefers the latter. Its object is to show at one view all the sides of each object; the classed catalogue shows together the same side of many objects.

There is not as yet much uniformity in catalogues nor does any carry out this principle so absolutely as the more obvious "specific" rule is obeyed. The Boston Public Library Supplement of 1866, for instance, has under the country *Antiquities, Coinage, Description* and *History, Language, Religion* (subjects), and *Literature* and even *Elocution* and *Poetry* (forms), but not *Ballads* nor *Periodicals,* which appear under those words. Yet when Ballads are called Volkslieder they appear under the country, Germany,—an instance of the independence of the title produced by foreign languages, the English title being entered by form-word, the foreign works having national classification, regardless of the title. There are many other classes that in most catalogues at present, instead of being confined to general works, absorb books which should rather have local entry, as **Vases, Gems, Sculpture, Painting,** and other branches of the fine arts, **Ballads, Epigrams, Plays,** and other forms of literature. In catalogues of merely English libraries this is perhaps as well (see § 88), but the multiplication of books and the accession of foreign literatures render more system necessary.

To show the procedure under this rule, suppose we have a collection of books on coins. Let the general works go under **Numismatics**; let works on any particular coin, as a Pine-tree shilling or a Queen Anne's farthing go under the name of the coin; let works on the coins of a country be put under its name; refer from the country to all the particular coins on which you have monographs, and from **Numismatics** both to all the separate coins and to all the countries on whose coinage you have treatises.

e. Between subjects that overlap.

69. Among subjects that overlap choose the one that preponderates, with a reference from the other.

Ex. Any complete treatise on domestic animals will cover a large part of the ground of veterinary medicine; but it is unnecessary to enter all the works on domestic animals under **Veterinary medicine** a note to this effect is sufficient. **Astronomy** and **Geology** overlap in regard to the origin of the earth, **Geology** and **Physical geography** in regard to its present condition. Any particular book must be classified with one or the other subject according as the geological or geographical treatment prevails.

2. Choice between different names.

General rules, always applicable, for the choice of names of subjects can no more be given than rules without exception in grammar. Usage in both cases is the supreme arbiter, — the usage, in the present case, not of the cataloguer but of the public in speaking of subjects.

f. Language.

70. When possible let the heading be in English, but a foreign word may be used when no English word expresses the subject of a book.

Ex. **Écorcheurs, Émigrés, Raskolnik.** Many terms of the Roman or civil law are not exactly translatable; neither Fault nor Crime gives the idea of Culpa, the Debitor inops is not our bankrupt or insolvent; he would have been very glad to have the privileges of a bankrupt. Some other technical terms and some names of bodies, sects, events should be left in the original language. The use of the Latin names of Greek deities (Jupiter, Neptune, Venus, in place of Zeus, Poseidon, Aphrodite) is a manifest inaccuracy. Yet it may be defended on the plea: (1) that the Latin names are at present more familiar to the majority of readers; (2) that it would be difficult to divide the literature, or if it were done, many books must be put both under Zeus and Jupiter, Poseidon and Neptune, etc., filling considerable room with no practical advantage.

g. Synonyms.

71. Of two exactly synonymous names choose one and make a reference from the other.

Ex. **Poisons** and **Toxicology**; **Antiquities** and **Archæology**; **Insects** and **Entomology**; **Warming** and **Heating**; **Pacific Ocean** and **South Sea**. There are some cases in which separate headings (**Hydraulics** and **Mechanics of Fluids**), which cannot be combined, cover books almost identical in character, so that the inquirer must look under both. This is an evil; but there is no reason for increasing the evil by separating headings that are really synonymous, certainly not for dividing a subject in this way for verbal causes and giving no hint that it has been divided.

It sometimes happens that a different name is given to the same subject at different periods of its history. When the method of study of the subject, or its objects, or the ideas connected with it, are very different at those two periods (as in the case of **Alchemy** and **Chemistry**) of course there must be two headings. There is not so much reason for separating Fluxions and Differential calculus, which differ only in notation. And there is no reason at all for separating **Natural Philosophy** and **Physics**. I am told that medical nomenclature has changed largely three times within the present century. How is the cataloguer, unless he happens to be a medical man, to escape occasionally putting works on one disease under three different heads?

To arrive at a decision in any case one must balance the advantages on the one hand of having all that relates to a subject together, and on the other of making that economical conjunction of title-entry and of subject-entry which comes from following the titles of the books in selecting names for their subjects.

In choosing between synonymous headings prefer the one that

(*a*) is most familiar to that class of people who consult the library; a natural history society will of course use the scientific name, a town library would equally of course use the popular name — **Butterflies** rather than **Lepidoptera**, **Horse** rather than **Equus caballus**. But the scientific may be preferable when the common name is ambiguous or of ill defined extent.

(*b*) is most used in other catalogues.

(*c*) has fewest meanings other than the sense in which it is to be employed.

(*d*) comes first in the alphabet, so that the reference from the other can be made to the exact page of the catalogue.

(*c*) brings the subject into the neighborhood of other related subjects. It is, for instance, often an advantage to have near any art or science the lives of those who have been famous in it, as **Art, Artists**; **Painters, Painting**; **Historians, History**. If one were hesitating between **Conjuring, Juggling, Legerdemain, Prestidigitation**, and **Sleight of hand**, it would be in favor of **Conjuring** or **Prestidigitation** that one could enter by their side **Conjurors** or **Prestidigitators**.

Sometimes one and sometimes another of these reasons must prevail. Each case is to be decided on its own merits.

72. In choosing between two names not exactly synonymous, consider whether there is difference enough to require separate entry; if not treat them as synonymous.

Ex. **Culture** and **Civilization, Culture** and **Education**.

73. Of two subjects exactly opposite choose one and refer from the other.

Ex. **Temperance** and **Intemperance, Free Trade** and **Protection, Authority** (in religion) and **Private judgment**. Reasons for choice the same as between synonyms.

To this rule there may be exceptions. It may be best that works on theism and atheism should be put together, perhaps under the heading **God**; but Theists and Atheists as bodies of religious believers ought certainly to go under those two headings, and therefore it is appropriate to put works in defence of theistic doctrines and those in defence of atheistic doctrines under **Theism** and **Atheism**.

h. Subject-word and subject.

74. Enter books under the word which best expresses their subject, whether it occurs in the title or not.

It is strange that the delusion ever should have arisen that "a catalogue must of necessity confine itself to titles only of books." If it does, it cannot enter that very considerable number of books whose titles make no mention or only an obscure or a defective mention of their subjects (§ 60), and it is at the mercy of deceptive titles (*e. g.*, Channing's sermon "On a future life," which treats of Heaven only, Irving's History of New York, Gulliver's Travels). A man who is looking up the history of the Christian church does not care in the least whether the books on it were called by their authors church histories or ecclesiastical histories; and the cataloguer also should not care if he can avoid it. The title rules the title-catalogue; let it confine itself to that province.

i. Homonyms.

75. Carefully separate the entries on different subjects bearing the same name, or take some other heading in place of one of the homonyms.

E. g., it will not do to confound works on the vegetable kingdom with works on vegetables, in the sense of kitchen-garden plants; the first would be properly entered under **Botany**. Special care is of course needed with foreign titles; the cataloguer may easily be misled by the sound if he is not on his guard. I have seen Lancelot's "Jardin des racines grecques" classed with works on **Gardening**, Stephanus Byzantinus "De Dodone [urbe Molossidis]" put under **Dodo** with a reference from **Ornithology**, and Garnier "Sur l'autorité paternelle" among the works on the Christian **Fathers**.

j. Compound subjects.

The name of a subject may be

(*a*) A single word as **Botany, Ethics**, or several words taken together, either

(*b*) A noun preceded by an adjective, as **Ancient history, Capital punishment, Moral philosophy**,

(*c*) A noun preceded by another noun used like an adjective, as **Death penalty, Flower fertilization**, (*d*) A noun connected with another by a preposition, as **Penalty of death, Fertilization of flowers,**

(*e*) A noun connected with another by "and," as **Ancients and moderns,**

(*f*) A sentence, as in the titles "Sur la règle **Paterna paternis materna maternis**" and "De usu paroemiae juris Germanici, **Der Letzte thut die Thüre zu**;" where the whole phrase would be the subject of the dissertation.

There are three main courses open:

(1) We can consider the subject to be the phrase *as it reads,* as **Agricultural chemistry, Survival of the fittest,** which is the only possible method in (*a*) and undoubtedly the best method in (*c*), (*e*), and (*f*), and in most cases of proper names, as **Democratic Party, White Mountains, Missouri River** (but see § 18).

(2) We can make our entry in (*b*), (*c*), and (*d*) under what we consider the most significant word of the phrase, inverting the order of the words if necessary; as **Probabilities** (instead of **Theory** of probabilities); **Earth,** Figure of the; **Species,** Origin of the, the word Origin here being by itself of no account; **Alimentary** canal, Canal being by itself of no account; **Political** economy, Political being here the main word and economy by itself having a meaning entirely different from that which it has in this connection.

(3) We can take the phrase as it reads in (*c*), (*d*), (*e*), and (*f*), but make a special rule for a noun preceded by an adjective (*b*), *first,* that all such phrases shall when possible be reduced to their equivalent nouns, as **Moral philosophy** to **Ethics** or to **Morals, Intellectual** or **Mental philosophy** to **Intellect** or **Mind, Natural philosophy** to **Physics, Sanitary science** to **Hygiene, Scientific men** to **Scientists, Social Science** to **Sociology**; and *secondly* that in all cases where such reduction is impossible the words shall be inverted and the noun taken as the heading, as **Chemistry,** Agricultural; **Chemistry,** Organic; **Anatomy,** Comparative; **History,** Ancient; **History,** Ecclesiastical; **History,** Modern; **History,** Natural; **History,** Sacred.*

The objection to (1) is that it may be pushed to an absurd extent in the case (*b*). A man might plausibly assert that Ancient Egypt is a distinct subject from Modern Egypt, having a recognized name of its own, as much so as Ancient history, and might therefore demand that the one should be put under **A** (Ancient) and the other under **M** (Modern);† and similar claims might be made in the case of all subject names to which an adjective is ever prefixed, which would result in filling the catalogue with a host of unexpected and therefore useless headings. Nevertheless the rule seems to me the best if due discrimination be used in choosing subject names.

The objection to (2) is that there would often be disagreement as to what is "the most important word of the phrase," so that the rule would be no guide to the reader. But in connection with (1) and as a guard against its excesses (2) has its value. The combined rule might read

76. Enter a compound subject-name by its first word, inverting the phrase only when some other word is decidedly more significant or is often used alone with the same meaning as the whole name.

Ex. **Special providences** and **Providence, Proper names** and **Names.**

It must be confessed that this rule is somewhat vague and that it would be often of doubtful application, and that on the other hand (3) is clear and easy to follow. But there are objections to (3). It would put a great many subjects under words where nobody unacquainted with the rule would expect to find them.

Works on the	would hardly be looked for under
Alimentary canal	Canal.
Dangerous classes	Classes.
Digestive organs	Organs.

* This rule is proposed by Mr. Schwartz and carried out, with some exceptions, in his catalogue of the New York Apprentices' Library.

† Which would be much like putting Williams's "Shakespeare's Youth" under Youthful Shakespeare. Individuals should not be divided.

Works on the	Would hardly be looked for under
Dispensing power	Power.
Domestic economy	Economy.
Ecclesiastical polity	Polity.
Final causes	Causes.
Gastric juice	Juice.
Laboring classes	Classes.
Military art	Art.
Parliamentary practice	Practice.
Political economy	Economy.
Solar system	System.
Suspended animation	Animation.
Zodiacal light	Light.

Another objection is that in most cases the noun expresses a class, the adjective limits the noun, and makes the name that of a subclass (as International law, Remittent diseases, Secret societies, Sumptuary laws, Typhoid fever, Venomous insects, Whig party, Woolen manufactures), and to adopt the noun (the class) as the heading is to violate the fundamental principle of the dictionary catalogue. The rule is urged, however, not on the ground of propriety or congruity with the rest of the system but simply as convenient, as a purely arbitrary rule which *once understood* will be a certain guide for the reader. "If he is told that he shall always find a subject arranged under its substantive form and never under an adjective he can hardly fail to find it. If, on the other hand, he is told that Comparative anatomy is under **C** and Morbid anatomy under **A**, that Physical geography is under **P** and Mathematical geography under **G**, he will only be bewildered, and accuse the cataloguer of making distinctions that it requires too much study to appreciate. Theoretically the distinctions may be justified, but practically the simpler way of using the noun only is more easily grasped by the common mind. And the system of classifying names under the surname is precisely analogous;* thus

Smith, John,
Smith, Joseph,
Smith, William,

seems to me to be arranged on the same principle as

History, Ancient,
History, Ecclesiastical,
History, Modern,
History, Sacred."†

This is plausible. If the public could ever get as accustomed to the inversion of subject-names as they are to the inversion of personal names the rule would undoubtedly be very convenient; but it might be difficult to teach the rule. The catalogue treatment of personal names is familiar to every one because it is used in all catalogues, dictionaries, directories, and indexes. But there are less than three hundred subject-names consisting of adjective and noun in a catalogue which has probably over 50,000 names of persons. The use of the rule would be so infrequent that it would not remain in the memory. And it should be observed that the confusion caused by the different treatment of Morbid anatomy and Comparative anatomy would only occur to a man who was examining the system of the catalogue, and not to the ordinary user. A man looks in the catalogue for treatises on **Comparative anatomy**; he finds it, where he first looks, under **C**. He does not know anything about the disposition of works on Morbid anatomy, and is not confused by it. Another man looks for works on Morbid anatomy and under **M** he is referred to **Anatomy**, *Morbid*.‡ He finds there what he wants and does not stop to notice that **Comparative anatomy** is not there, but under **C**, consequently he is not puzzled by that. And even those who are taking a

* But if analogies are to have any weight, why should we follow that of names of persons, which are inverted, more than that of names of places, which are not? We do not say **Mountains**, White; **Regions**, Antarctic; **Sea**, Red; why should we say **Anatomy**, Comparative: **Arts**, Fine; **System**, Brunonian? — C.

† Schwartz, slightly altered.

‡ This is on the supposition that Morbid Anatomy has been considered by the cataloguer not to be a distinct subject, entitled to a name of its own.

general survey of all that the library possesses on anatomy would probably be too intent upon their object to pause and criticise the arrangement, provided the reference from **Anatomy** to **Comparative Anatomy** were perfectly clear, so that they ran no risk of overlooking it and had no difficulty in finding the subject referred to.

The specific-entry rule is one which the reader of a dictionary catalogue must learn if he is to use it with any facility; it is much better that he should not be burdened with learning an exception to this, which the noun rule certainly is.

It ought also to be noticed that this plan does not escape all the difficulties of the others. In reducing, for instance, Intellectual philosophy or Moral philosophy, will you say Mind or Intellect, Morals or Ethics? And the reader will not always know what the equivalent noun is,—that Physics = Natural Philosophy, for example, and Hygiene = Sanitary science. Nor does it help us at all to decide whether to prefer Botanical morphology or Morphological botany. These difficulties, which beset any rule, are only mentioned here lest too much should be expected from a plan which at first sight seems to solve all problems.

The practice of reducing a name to the substantive form is often a good one; but should not be insisted upon as an invariable rule, as it might lead to the adoption of some very out-of-the-way names. As a mere matter of form Nebulæ is to be preferred for a heading to Nebular hypothesis, Pantheism to Pantheistic theory, Lyceums to Lyceum system, etc.

In (*b*), (*c*), and (*d*) the same subject can often be named in different ways, as

(*b*) **Capital punishment.**	**Floral fertilization.**
(*c*) **Death penalty.**	**Flower fertilization.**
(*d*) **Penalty of death.**	**Fertilization of flowers.**

Is there any principle upon which the choice between these three can be made, so that the cataloguer shall always enter books on the same subject under the same heading? I see none. When there is any decided usage (*i. e.*, custom of the public to designate the subjects by one of the names rather than by the others) let it be followed; that is to say, if, in the examples given above, the more customary phrases are **Capital punishment, Fertilization of flowers,** then we must use those names, preferring in the first case the name which begins with an adjective to its equivalent beginning with a noun, and in the other the name beginning with a noun to its equivalent beginning with an adjective. As is often the case in language usage will be found not to follow any uniform course.

If usage manifests no preference for either name, we cannot employ the two indifferently; we must choose one; and some slight guide to choice in certain cases may perhaps be found. On examination of the phrases above it appears that they are not all of the same composition. In **Comparative anatomy, Capital punishment** the noun is the name of a general subject, one of whose subdivisions is indicated by the adjective. And Capital, Comparative have only this limiting power, they do not imply any general subject. But **Ancient history, Mediæval history,** etc., may be viewed not only in this way (History the class, Ancient history and Mediæval history the subdivisions) but also as equivalent to **Antiquity:** *History*, **Middle Ages:** *History* (as we say **Europe:** *History*), in which case the adjectives (Ancient, Mediæval) imply a subject and the noun (History) indicates the aspect in which the subject is viewed. Here then we choose **Ancient** and **Mediæval** as the heading on the principle of § 63. So in (*b*) and (*c*) each of the nouns in turn may be considered as expressing the more general idea and the other as limiting it; *e. g.*, we can have various headings for Death considered in different lights, among others as a penalty; and we can have headings of various sorts of penalties, among others death. It is evident that this collection of penalties taken together makes up a class, and therefore this belongs to a style of entry which the dictionary catalogue is expected to avoid; but the series of headings beginning with the word Death would not make a class, being merely different aspects of the same thing, not different subordinate parts of the same subject.

When an adjective implies the name of a place, as in **French literature, German philosophy, Greek art,** it is most convenient on the whole to make the subject a division under the country. In this way all that relates to a country is brought together and arranged in one alphabetical series of subjects under its name (see § 201). It is not of the slightest importance that this introduces the *appearance* of an alphabetico-classed catalogue, so long as the main object of a dictionary, ready reference, is attained. Of course **Hebrew language, Latin language, Latin literature,** and **Punic language** cannot be so treated; it is the custom and is probably best not to put **English language** and **English literature** under **England,** as they have extended far beyond the place of their origin; books on the lngauage spoken in the United States go with those on the English language except the few on **Americanisms,** which are separated, like accounts of any other dialect. Our literature cannot be treated satisfactorily. It is never called United States literature and no one would expect to find it under United States. On the other hand the name American properly should include Canadian literature and all the Spanish literature of South America. It is however the best name we have.

k. Double entry.

It is plain that almost every book will appear several times in the catalogue:

Under author, if he is known.

Under first word of title, if the book is anonymous or the title is memorable.

Under each distinct subject.

Under form-heading in many cases.

Under many other headings by way of cross-reference.

And this is necessary if the various objects enumerated on p. 10 are to be attained quickly. But inasmuch as the extent and therefore the cost of the catalogue increases in direct proportion with the multiplication of entries it becomes worth while to inquire whether some of these cannot be dispensed with by devices which will suit the inquirer as well or nearly as well. Such economies are mentioned in §§ 67, 68, 80, 81.

77. Enter a polytopical book under each distinct subject.

Ex. "An art journey in **Italy** and **Greece**;" "The history of **France** and **England** compared;" "Handbook of **drawing** and **engraving.**"

But some of the subjects may be omitted if their treatment is so slight that it is not worth while to take any notice of them, which is occasionally the case even when they are mentioned on the title-page. Sometimes an analytical can take the place of a full entry for the less important topics. The points to be considered are: (1) Would this book be of any use to one who is looking up this subject? (2) Is the entry or reference necessary as a subject-word entry or reference (that is, to one who is looking for this book)?

Some books are polytopical which do not appear to be so at first sight. A collection of portraits of Germans, for example, has the subject **Germans,** and so far as it has any artistic value might be quoted as one of the illustrative works under the subject **Portrait painting** or **Portrait engraving.*** If the biographical interest were all, the general collections would be put under **Portraits** and the national collections (as "American portrait gallery," "Zwei Hundert Bildnisse deutscher Männer") under countries, with references from the general heading to the various countries, as directed in § 68. If the artistic interest were alone considered, the general titles would be put under **Portraits,** and collections by painters or engravers of particular schools would be put under the names of the schools; which would amount to nearly the same arrangement as the previous.

So in regard to **Hymns**; there are three sources of interest, the devotional, the literary (which would lead to national subdivision), and the denominational; a similar treatment would place general collections under **Hymns,** collections in any language under the national heading, with either double entry under the name of the denomination or a reference from that to the national heading, specifying which of the collections there enumerated belong to the denomination. But the devotional interest so decidedly preponderates that it may be best to collect everything under the form-heading **Hymns,** which also has the advantage of being the usual one.

In Full, almanacs will have form-entry under **Almanacs** and subject-entry under the district about which they give information.

Sometimes if an ordinary reference be made from one subject to another the title referred to

* It also belongs to the class Portraits, but that is in the Form-catalogue, not the Subject-catalogue.

cannot easily be found. A reference from **Architecture** to **Spain**: *Architecture,* is convenient, but a reference to the same heading from **Gothic architecture** is not, because it obliges the inquirer to look through the whole list of Spanish architecture to find perhaps one title on the Gothic. In like manner there would be few entries of works on vases under most countries, so that no division *Vases* would be made, and the inquirer must search for his book among a number of titles on *Art.* And if the reference were made the other way—from the country to **Vases**—the inquirer would be in the same plight. There is no need however of double entry. If merely the name of the particular author or authors referred to under any subject be inserted in the reference, the whole difficulty vanishes.

Ex. **Gothic architecture.** [Various titles.] *See also* **Spain**: *Architecture* (STREET).

It is to be noted that herein Short has a great advantage; it does not lose so much by double entry and can afford to make it in many cases where Medium must for economy put the reader to some trouble. The notes, too, in such catalogues as the Quincy or the Boston Public history-list afford a convenient way of briefly inserting considerable double entry where it is thought expedient without any apparent inconsistency.

78. If a book purports to treat of several subjects, which together make the whole or a great part of one more general, it may be put either under each of the special subjects, or under the general subject, and in the latter case it may or may not have analytical references from the specific subjects, according as the treatises are more or less distinct and more or less important.

E. g., "A treatise on anatomy, physiology, pathology, and therapeutics," which might be put under each of those four headings, ought rather to be entered under **Medicine**, in which case, if the separate parts are by different authors, analyticals might very well be made under the four headings; and at any rate an analytical under the first would occasionally be useful as equivalent to a subject-word reference.

79. When a considerable number of books might all be entered under the same two or more headings, entry under one will be sufficient, with a reference from the others.

On the other hand, if in printing it were noticed that under any subject only one or two titles were covered by the cross-references to countries (as from **Sculpture** to **Greece, Italy, Denmark**), it may be thought that double entry under nation and subject would be preferable. A man is provoked if he turns to another part of the catalogue to find there only one title. However it should be remembered that one or two titles repeated under each of many subjects will amount to a considerable number in the whole. The want of uniformity produced by this mixture of reference and double entry is of less importance.

79½. When there are many editions of a book it is allowable to merely refer under the subject to the author-entry. In a college library, for instance, the full entry of all the editions of the classics under their appropriate subjects (as of the Georgics under **Agriculture**, of Thucydides under **Greek history**, and Polybius under **Roman history**), would be a waste of room; it is enough to mention the best edition and refer for other editions and translations to the author's name.

l. Miscellaneous rules and examples.

80. Trials relating to a vessel should be put under its name; Short would make no other entry. Exploring expeditions or voyages in a named vessel should have at least a reference from the name.

Ex. **Jeune Eugénie.** MASON, W. P. Report. Boston, 1822. 8°.

Herald, *H. M. S*, Voyage of the. *See* **Seemann, B.**

81. A civil action is to be entered under that party to it who is first named on the title-page, with a reference from the other.

In Short (and in Medium and Full, if the report is anonymous) this will be the only entry,—unless the case illustrate some subject, in which case entry or reference under that will be needed. Patent cases furnish the most common examples of subject-entry of trials, but everyone will remember trials in which points of ecclesiastical law, of medical jurisprudence, etc., have been so fully discussed as to compel reference from those subjects.

82. Enter "Review of," "Remarks on," "Comments on" under the author reviewed (as a combined subject and subject-word entry), and, if worth while, under the subject of the book reviewed.

83. The distinction between **Bibliography** and **Literary history** is, with reference to the books on those subjects, a distinction of more or less; the two classes of books run into each other and it is hard to draw the line between them.

84. Any theological library will probably contain books which treat

(1) of the four last things, death, judgment, heaven, and hell.

(2) of the nature of the life after death, a much more extensive question than (1).

(3) whether there is any future life, without regard to its nature.

(4) of the retribution after death for the good and for the evil deeds done in this life.

(5) whether there is any retribution for evil in a future life.

(6) what is its nature.

(7) how long does it last.

Here are seven questions on nearly the same subject-matter, and there are six names for them. (It will be found, by the way, that although there are some books treating of each separately, many of the works overlap as the subjects do, and that the titles are no guide whatever to the contents of the books.) Two main courses are open to the cataloguer:

1st. To make one heading, as **Future life**, cover the whole, with subdivisions. In this way the catalogue becomes classed to a certain extent. No matter if that is, on the whole, the more convenient arrangement,

2d. More consistently, to make four headings: **Eschatology** (covering the 1st question, four last things, with references to each of them), **Future life** (its nature, including retribution both for good and evil, 2d and 4th question), **Future punishment** (existence, nature, duration, and so including universalism, with references to Purgatory and Hell, covering the 5th, 6th, and 7th questions), **Immortality** (is there any? 3d question).

B. Entries considered as parts of a whole.

The systematic catalogue undertakes to exhibit a scientific arrangement of the books in a library in the belief that it will thus best aid those who would pursue any extensive or thorough study. The dictionary catalogue sets out with another object and a different method, but having attained that object—facility of reference—is at liberty to try to secure some of the advantages of classification and system in its own way. Its subject-entries, individual, general, limited, extensive, thrown together without any logical arrangement, in most absurd proximity—**Abscess** followed by **Absenteeism** and that by **Absolution**, **Club-foot** next to **Clubs**, and **Communion** to **Communism**, while **Christianity** and **Theology**, **Bibliography** and **Literary history** are separated by half the length of the catalogue—are a mass of utterly disconnected particles without any relation to one another, each useful in itself but only by itself. But by a well-devised network of cross-references the mob becomes an army of which each part is capable of assisting many other parts. The effective force of the catalogue is immensely increased.

85. Make references from general subjects to their various subordinate subjects and also to co-ordinate and illustrative subjects.

Cross-references should be made by Full from Classes of persons (Merchants, Lawyers, Artists, Quakers, etc.) to individuals belonging to those classes; from Cities to persons connected with them by birth or residence or at least to those who have taken part in the municipal affairs or rendered the city illustrious; from Countries to their colonies, provinces, counties, cities, etc. (unless their number is so great or the divisions are so well known that reference is useless); also, under the division *History* to rulers and statesmen, under *Literature* to authors, under *Art* to artists, and so on; from other Subjects to all their parts, and to the names of persons distinguished for discoveries in them or knowledge of them. Short and Medium will make such of these references as seem most likely to be useful.

The construction of this system may be carried on simultaneously with the ordinary cataloguing of the library, each book as it goes through the cataloguer's hands not merely receiving its author- and subject-entries, but also suggesting the appropriate cross-reference; but when all the books are catalogued the system will not be complete. References are needed not merely to the specific from the general but to the general from the more general and to that from the most general; there must be a pyramid of references, and this can be made only by a final revision after the completion of the cataloguing. The best method is to draw off in a single column a list of all the subject-headings that have been made, to write opposite them their including classes in a second column and the including classes of these in a third column; then to write these classes as headings to cards and under them the subjects that stood respectively opposite to them in the list, to arrange the cards alphabetically, verify the references, and supplement them by thinking of all likely subordinate headings and ascertaining whether they are in the catalogue, and also by considering what an inquirer would like to be told or reminded of if he were looking up the subject under consideration. In this way a reasonably complete list may be made.

It will, however, often happen that there is no entry under the including subject. Take a simple instance. The catalogue, we will suppose, contains twenty histories of towns belonging to seven counties in Connecticut. In the revision described above references have been made both from Connecticut *to* these counties and to the towns *from* the counties, but only three of the counties have any titles under them. The others would not make their appearance in the catalogue at all if there were no cross-references. And as this will happen continually it follows that the system will very greatly increase the number of headings and therefore the length of the catalogue. Such fullness may be allowable in regard to the state which contains the library, which of course should be treated with exceptional completeness; it may possibly be worth while for all the states of the Union and for England, but to attempt to do the same for all countries and all subjects is too much. A modification of the plan must be introduced, which will make it much less complete but still useful. With many subjects the next heading in the ascending series must be skipped, and the references massed under one still higher; in the supposed case, for example, the references to all the towns will be made under Connecticut and under those counties alone which have any other entry under them.

86. Make references occasionally from specific to general subjects.

Of course much information about limited topics is to be found in more general works; the very best description of a single plant or of a family of plants may perhaps be contained in a botanical encyclopædia. This fact, however, must be impressed upon the inquirer in the preface of the catalogue or in a printed card giving directions for its use; it is out of the question to make all possible references of the ascending kind. From **Cathedrals**, for example, one would naturally refer to **Christian art** and to **Ecclesiastical architecture**, because works on those subjects will contain more or less on cathedrals. But so will histories of architecture and histories of English, French, German, or Spanish architecture; so will travels in England, France, Germany, Italy, Spain. And anyone who desired to take an absolutely complete survey of the subject, or who was willing to spend unlimited time in getting information on some detail, would have to consult such books. Yet the cataloguer may very excusably not think of referring to those subjects, or if he thinks of it may deem the connection too remote to justify reference, and that he should be overloading the catalogue with what would be generally useless.

There are many things that are seldom used, and then perhaps but for an instant, and yet their existence is justified because when wanted they are indispensable or because they make useful what is otherwise useless: a policy of insurance, life-preservers in a steamer, the index of a book, large parts of the catalogue of a library, among others the cross-references. Of such a nature, but much less useful, more easily dispensed with, is a

87. Synoptical table of subjects.

I mention its possibility here; I do not advise its construction, because there is little chance that the result would compensate for the immense labor.

IV. FORM-ENTRY.

National entry has already been discussed under SUBJECTS (§68).

88. Make a form-entry for collections of works in any form of literature.

In the catalogues of libraries consisting chiefly of English books, if it is thought most convenient to make form-entries under the headings **Poetry, Drama, Fiction,** it may be done, because for those libraries Poetry is synonymous with English poetry, and so on; but if a library has any considerable number of books in foreign languages the national classification should be strictly followed; that is to say, entries should be made under **English drama, English fiction, English poetry, Latin poetry,** etc.; only those collections of plays, novels, poems that include specimens of several literatures being put under **Drama, Fiction, Poetry**. Or the English plays, novels, poems, *etc.*, may be entered under Drama, Fiction, Poetry, *etc.*, and the dramatic works, *etc.*, of foreign literatures under the names of the several literatures.

The rule above confines itself to collections. It would be convenient to have full lists of the single works in the library in all the various kinds of literature, and when space can be afforded they ought to be given; if there is not room for them, references must be made under these headings to the names of all the single authors; an unsatisfactory substitute it is true, but better than entire omission. Note, however, that there is much less need of these lists in libraries which give their frequenters access to the shelves than where such access is denied, so that borrowers must depend entirely on the catalogue. In the case of English fiction a form-list is of such constant use that nearly all libraries have separate fiction catalogues.

It has been objected that such lists of novels, plays, etc., do not suit the genius of the dictionary catalogue. The objection is of no importance if true; if such lists are useful they ought to be given. There is nothing in the dictionary plan which makes them hard to use if inserted. But the objection is not well founded. Under the names of certain subjects we give lists of the authors who have treated of those subjects; under the names of certain kinds of literature we give lists of the authors who have written books in those forms; the cases are parallel. The divisions of fiction, it must be understood, are not the authors who have written novels but the different kinds of novels which they have written; they are either such varieties as "Historical fiction," "Sea stories," "Religious novels," or such as "English fiction," "French fiction." The first divisions we do not make for single works because it would be very difficult to do so and of little use; but if there were collections in those classes we should certainly introduce such headings. The second division (by language) is made as it is in Poetry and Drama, both for single works and collections.

There is no reason but want of room why only collections should be entered under form-headings. The first entries of collections were merely title-entries and Mr. Crestadoro is the only person who has thought that plays, etc., deserve two title-entries, one from the first word the other from what we might call the form-word. It is not uninteresting to watch the steps by which the fully organized quadruple syndetic dictionary catalogue is gradually developing from the simple subject-word index.

89. Make a form-entry for single works in the rarer literatures, as Japanese, or Kalmuc, or Cherokee.

References can be substituted, if necessary.

90. Make a form-entry of encyclopædias, indexes, and works of similar practical form, the general ones under the headings **Encyclopædias**, etc., the special ones in groups under their appropriate subjects.

Thus an agricultural dictionary will not be entered under **Dictionaries**, but under **Agriculture**, in a little division *Dictionaries*. Now and then some one asks for "a grammar," "the dictionary." It does not follow that it would be well to jumble together, under a form-heading **Grammars** or **Dictionaries**, all grammars and lexicons in all languages. Those who inquire so vaguely must be made to state their wishes more definitely. The cataloguer does his part if he inserts a note under such headings explanatory of the practice of the catalogue; as

Grammar. [First a list of works on general grammar, then]

Note. For grammars of any language see the name of the language.

V. ANALYSIS.

91. Enter in full every work, forming part of a set, which fills a whole volume or several volumes.

Ex. **Colombo**, C. Select letters rel. to his four voyages to the New World; tr. and ed. by R. H. Major. London, 1847. 8°. (Vol. 2 of the Hakluyt Soc.)

92. Enter analytically, that is without imprint,

a. every work, forming part of a set, which has a separate title-page and paging, but forms only part of a volume of the set.

Ex. **Fairholt**, F. W. The civic garland; songs from London pageants, with introd. and notes. (*In* **Percy Society**, v. 19, 1845.)

Full must and Medium may make a full entry in this case also. That is to say, Full will draw the line at a separate title-page, Short and perhaps Medium at filling a volume. Those catalogues which give no imprints at all and those which give no imprints under subjects will of course give none for analyticals.

b. Every work which, though not separately paged or not having a title-page, has been published separately, whether before or since its publication in the work under treatment.

Ex. **Dickens**, C. J. F. Little Dorrit. (*In* **Harper's** mag., v. 12-15, 1855-57.)

c. Under *author*, (1) every separate article or treatise over [1] pages in length; (2) treatises of noted authors; (3) noted works even if by authors otherwise obscure.

[1] This limit must be determined by each library for itself, with the understanding that there may be occasional exceptions.

d. Under *subject* treatises important either (1) as containing the origin of a science or a controversy or developing new views, or (2) as treating the subject ably or giving important information, or (3) for length.

Absolute uniformity is unattainable; probably no one will be able to draw the line always at the same height. It is most desirable — and fortunately easiest — to make analysis when the subject is well marked, as of biographies or histories of towns, or monographs on any subject. General treatises or vague essays are much harder to classify and much less valuable for analysis. In analyzing collections of essays original articles should be brought out in preference to reviews, which are commonly not worth touching (except in a very full catalogue) either under the author of the work reviewed or under its subject. Of course exception may be made for famous reviews or for good reviews of famous works. A work giving careful literary estimate of an author may be an exception to this remark; reviews of the "Works" of any author are most likely to contain such an estimate. Many reviews, like Macaulay's, are important for their treatment of the subject and not worth noticing under the book reviewed, which is merely a pretext for the article.

Make analytical title-references for stories in a collection when they are likely to be inquired for separately.

93. Make analyticals for the second and subsequent authors of a book written (*but not conjointly*) by several authors. (See § 3.)

Sometimes it is better to give full entry under two headings than to make the second analytical. *Ex.* A "Short account of the application to Parliament by the merchants of London, with the substance of the evidence as summed up by Mr. Glover," is to be entered under **London.** *Merchants,* as first author, but as Glover's part is two-thirds of the whole, it should also be entered under him, the entry in each case being made full enough not to mislead.

In analyticals it is well, though not necessary, to give the date of the book referred to and the pages which contain the article. Many readers will not notice these details but they will do no one any harm and will assist the careful student.

VI. STYLE.

A. Headings.

Type, 94–98. Italics, 95. Pseud., 99, 100. Ed., 101. Family name, 102. Christian name, 103, 104. To distinguish authors of the same name, 103, 105. To distinguish subject headings, 106. Dashes, 107. References, 108.

B. Titles.

Order, 109. Abridgement, 110–119. Articles, 110, 111. Unnecessary words, 112, 113. Dates, 114. Initials, 115. Abbreviations, 116. Numbers, 117. Position, 118. "Same," 119. Words to be retained, 120–124. Analyticals, 124. Exact copying, 125. Language, 126, 127. Translations, 127, 128. Transposition of the article, 129. Anon., 130, 131. Lord, Gen., ed., 132. Transliteration, 133.

C. Editions, 134, 135.

D. Imprints.

The parts of an imprint and their order, 136. Transliteration, 137. Abbreviations, 138. Two or more places, 139, 140. Publisher's name, 141. Colophon, 142. Dates, 142–152. Number of volumes, 153. Typographical form, 154.

E. Contents, 155–157, and Notes, 158.

F. References, 159, 160.

G. Capitals, 161, 162.

H. Punctuation, Accents, Italics, *etc.*, 163–168.

I. Arrangement.

Order of the English alphabet, 169. Headings, 170–185. Person, place, title, subject, form, 170. Christian names, 171, 172. M', *etc.*, 173. Same names, 174, 175. Titles, Sees, 176. Possessive case, 177. Greek and Latin names, 178. Compound names, 179–183. Pseudonyms, 184. Abbreviations, 185. Titles, 186–196. Under an author, 186–193. Editions, 188. Numerals, 189. Translations, 190. Biographies, etc., 191. Criticisms, 192. Analyticals, 193. Under countries, 194–196. Contents, 197. Subjects, 198–202. Homonyms, 198. Topical arrangement, 199. Chronological arrangement, 200. Cross-references, 201. Divisions, 202.

J. Etc.

Supplement, 203. An economy, 204. Incunabula and other rare books, 205.

STYLE.

Uniformity for its own sake is of very little account; for the sake of intelligibility, to prevent perplexity and misunderstanding, it is worth something. And it is well to be uniform merely to avoid the question "Why were you not consistent?"

A. HEADINGS.

94. Print headings in some marked type.

Either heavy-faced (best, if it can be had not too black), small capitals (handsome), or italics (least pleasing); never capitals (ugly and hard to read). Christian names should be in ordinary type; to make them like the heading is confusing, to have a special type for them would be extravagant.

95. Italicize titles of honor and similar distinguishing words.

Earl, Mrs., Rev., of Paris, Alexandrinus, etc., also the name of a country or state following the name of a town, as Wilton, *N. H.*, Cambridge, *Eng.* ☞ These words are to be italicized only in the headings and not in the title. They are italicized in the heading to distinguish the name and bring it out clearly; there is no need of such distinction in titles. Do not print **Badeau,** *Gen.* A. Life of *Gen.* Grant. If the heading is italicized, the words *Mrs., Earl,* &c., must be distinguished from it in some other way.

96. Print the headings of all the four kinds of entry (author, title, subject, form) in the same kind of type.

In some indexes a distinction is made between persons and places or between authors and subjects, but in a catalogue varieties of type must be reserved for more important distinctions. The Catalogue of the Library of the Interior Department uses a heavy-faced title type for authors and a light-faced antique for other entries, with very satisfactory effect; but such typographical luxuries are not within general reach.

97. Print the whole of an author-, title-, or form-heading in the special type; also an alternative family name and the family name of the second of joint authors.

Ex. **Cervantes Saavedra, Varnhagen von Ense, Cape of Good Hope, Bicknell & Goodhue, American Antiquarian Society, Comparative anatomy, Political economy; Chasteillon** (*Lat.* **Castalio** *or* **Castellio**), S.; **Craik,** G. L., *and* **Knight,** C.

98. Print the first word of a title-entry in the special type.

Ex. **Rough** diamond. But compound words, whether hyphened or not, should be printed wholly in the heading type, as **Out of door** amusements. London, 1834. 8°. This is merely for looks; the kind of type has nothing to do with the arrangement.

99. Add *pseud.* to the heading for all sorts of false names of whatever origin.

So much is necessary to prevent mistake on the part of the public; but it is a waste of time for the cataloguer to rack his brains to discover which of the ingenious names invented by Pierquin de Gembloux (cryptonym, geonym, phrenonym, etc.) is applicable to each case; for the only result is that readers are puzzled. A list of these terms may be found in the Notice of Quérard by Olphar Hamst [*i. e.*, R. Thomas], London, 1867. The unauthorized assumption of any name should be indicated by such phrases as *called, calling himself, dit, soi-disant, se dicente* or *che si dice, que se dice* or *se dicendiose, genannt, genoemd,* etc.

100. When an author habitually uses a pseudonym add it to his name; when the pseudonym is used only in one work, and different ones in other works, include it in that title, followed by [*pseud.*].

Ex. **Clemens**, S. C. (*pseud.* Mark **Twain**).
Godwin, Wm. The looking-glass; by T. Marcliffe [*pseud.*].

101. Add *ed.* to the heading when it is needed to show that a book is merely put together not written by the author in hand.

The title usually shows this fact clearly enough without *ed.* Short would omit to note the fact and in Full, perhaps even in Medium, it is better to state it in the title than in the heading. The distinction, after all, is rarely of practical value.

102. Repeat the family name for each person.

Ex.		
Smith, Caleb. Sermon.	not	**Smith**, Caleb. Sermon.
Smith, Charles. Address..		——, Charles. Address.
Smith, Conrad. Narrative.		——, Conrad. Narrative.

103. Distinguish authors whose family name is the same by giving the Christian name in full or by initials.

In a card catalogue the names should always be given in full, in printing initials are often used to save room; but the saving is small, and the advantages of full names are so considerable that any cataloguer who is relieved from the necessity of the greatest possible compression ought to give them. Under subjects however it is rare that two persons of even the same family name come together and initials are sufficient. An exception may well be made in the case of men always known by a double name, as Sydney Smith or Bayard Taylor. Nobody talks of Smith or Taylor. **Taylor**, B. (or in full J. B.) conveys no idea whatever to most readers; **Taylor**, J. Bayard, they know. When one name alone is usual, as Gladstone, Shakespeare, or both forms are used, as Dickens and Charles Dickens, initials will suffice. Of course there can be no uniformity in such practice, but there will be utility, which is better.

104. Mark in some way those Christian names which are usually omitted by the author.

Ex. **Collins**, (Wm.) Wilkie; **Gérard**, (Cécile) Jules (Basile). This is of practical use. The consulter running over the Collinses is puzzled by the unusual name unless some generally accepted sign shows him that it is unusual. He does not quickly recognize Charles Dickens in **Dickens**, Charles John Huffam; or Leigh Hunt in **Hunt**, James Henry Leigh; or Bayard Taylor in **Taylor**, James Bayard. Besides the eye finds the well-known name more quickly if the others are as it were pushed aside. The most common methods of distinction are inclosure in parentheses and spacing: **Guizot**, (François Pierre) Guillaume, or **Guizot**, F r a n ç o i s P i e r r e Guillaume. The latter is objectionable as unusual, as taking too much room, and as making emphatic the very part of the name which one wants to hide. But in those catalogues in which all Christian names are enclosed in parentheses, some other sign must of course be used to mark the less usual names.

105. Distinguish authors whose family and Christian names are the same by the dates of their birth and death, or, if these are not known, by some other label.

Ex. Bp., C.E., Capt., Col., D.D., F.R.S., etc., always to be printed in italics.

In a manuscript catalogue, in preparing which of course one never knows how many new names may be added, such titles should be given to every name. In printing, if room is an object, they may be omitted except when needed for the distinction of synonymous authors. Note, however, that many persons are commonly known and spoken of by a title rather than by their first name, and it is a convenience for the man who is looking, for instance, for the life of Gen. Greene, whose Christian name he does not know, to see at once, as he runs his eye over the list of Greenes, which are generals, without having to read all the titles of books written by or about the Greenes in order to identify him. For the same reason *Mrs.* should always be given with the name of a married woman, whether the Christian name which follows is her own or her husband's; unless the following form is adopted, "**Hall**, Anna Maria

(Fielding), *wife of* S. C.," which is always to be done when in her titles she uses her husband's initials. In this case a reference should be made from **Hall**, *Mrs.* S. C., to **Hall**, A. M., and so in similar cases. If Christian names are represented under subjects by their initials, it is well to give *Miss* or *Mrs.* with the names of female authors. The reader who would like to read a book by Miss Cobbe on a certain subject may not feel sure that **Cobbe**, F. P., is Miss Cobbe.

Distinctive epithets to be in English, as *Bishop of Meaux, Emperor of Germany,* excepting patronymics habitually joined with a person's name, as **Clemens** *Alexandrinus.*

Prefixes (*i. e.*, titles which in speaking come before the name), as *Hon., Mrs., Rev.,* etc., should be placed before the Christian name (as **Smith**, *Capt.* John), and suffixes, as *Jr., D.D., LL.D.*, after it (as **Channing**, James Ellery, *D.D.*). Hereditary titles generally follow the Christian name, as **Stanley**, Thomas, *1st Earl of Derby;* but British courtesy titles (*i. e.*, those given to the younger sons of dukes and marquesses) precede, as **Wellesley**, *Lord* Charles (2d son of the Duke of Wellington). English patronymic phrases, as *of Dedham*, follow, as do foreign ones; but they must immediately follow the family name when they are always used in close connection with it, as **Girault** *de St. Farjeau*, Eusèbe; similarly *aîné, fils, jeune,* as **Dumas** *fils*, Alexandre; **Didot** *fils*, Ambroise. Latin appellatives should not in general be separated from their nouns by a comma, as **Cæsar** *Heisterbacensis.*

106. Distinguish two subject-headings which are spelled alike by italicized phrases in parentheses.

Ex. **Calculus** (*in mathematics*).
Calculus (*in medicine*).

107. Medium avoids the repetition of the heading with all titles after the first by using a dash. Short usually employs indention.

Indention takes as much room as the dash and is much less clear. There should always be at least a hair-space between the end of the dash and the next letter; indeed that is the rule of all good printing. Under a subject the repetition of the author's name is indicated by a second dash.

Cobbett, Wm. Emigrant's guide.
— Grammar of English.
— Porcupine's works.

Atheism. BEECHER, L. Lectures, *etc.*
— BENTLEY, R. Confutation of A.
— — Folly of A. and deism.

108. Print in the special type a heading occurring in other parts of the catalogue, when a reference is intended.

After *See* or *In*, or when in a note some book contained in the catalogue is referred to, as "For a discussion of the authorship, *see* **Graesse's** Lehrbuch."

B. Titles.

1. Order.

109. Preserve the order of words of the title.

Short will depart from the order whenever it cannot otherwise abridge the title; Medium and Full will do the same, but they will bracket all words introduced out of their original place as much as if they did not occur in the title at all.

2. Abridgement.

The more careful and studentlike the probable use of the library the fuller the title should be,—fuller, that is, of information not of words. Many a title a yard long does not convey as much meaning as two well chosen words. No precise rule can be given for abridgement. The title must not be so much shortened that the book shall be confounded with any other book of the same author or any other edition of the same book, or that it shall fail to be recognized by those who know it or have been referred to it by title, or that it shall convey a false or insufficient idea of the nature of the work and (under the subject) of its theme and its method of treating its theme.[1] On the other hand it must not retain anything which could reasonably be inferred from the rest of the title or from its position under a given heading.[2]

[1] This clause must be very differently interpreted according to the character of the catalogue. It expresses rather the object to be aimed at than the point which an ordinary catalogue can expect to reach. To fully describe and characterize every book is impossible for most cataloguers. Still by a little management much may be briefly done. The words drama, play, novel, historical novel, poem, retained from or inserted in the title tell a great deal in a little space.

[2] It must make these omissions not merely that the catalogue may be short but that consulting it may be easy. Other things being equal that title is best which can be taken in at a glance. What has been said in defense of full titles may be true, that "it takes longer to abridge a title than to copy it in full," but it is also true that it takes longer for the printer to set the unabridged title, and longer for the reader to ascertain its meaning, and a long-title catalogue besides being more expensive is more bulky and therefore less convenient.

110. Omit the preliminary article when it can be done without altering the sense or too much offending the ear.

It will not do even for Short to catalogue "On the true, the beautiful and the good" thus:

Cousin, V. True, beautiful, good;

but a list of Buckstone's plays may as well be printed

— Breach of promise, comedy.
— Christening, farce.
— Dead shot, farce.
— Dream at sea.
— Kiss in the dark, farce.
— Lesson for ladies, com.

though the meaning of "Christening" and "The christening" is slightly different, and "Kiss in the dark" might be taken for an injunction, whereas "A kiss in the dark" is evidently only a title. Still neither Short nor Medium should hesitate to omit even in these cases. Besides the economy, the alphabetical order is brought out more clearly by this omission. That can also be done awkwardly by transposing the article, as

— Breach of promise, The; com.
— Christening, The; farce.
— Dead shot, The; farce.
— Dream at sea, The.

111. Short omits articles in the title.

Ex. "Observations upon an alteration of the charter of the Bank of England," is abridged: "Alteration of charter of Bank of England," which is certainly not euphonious, but is as intelligible as if it were. Medium usually indulges in the luxury of good English. Perhaps in time a catalogue style will be adopted in which these elisions shall be not merely allowed, but required. It may be possible to increase the number of cataloguing signs. We have now 8° where we once had octavo, then 8vo. Why not insist upon N. Y. for New York, L. for London, P. for Paris, etc., as a few adventurous libraries have done. Why not make free substitution of commas for words, and leave out articles and prepositions in titles wherever the sense will still remain gleanable?

112. Omit puffs[1] and many descriptive words which are implied either by the rest of the title[2] or by the custom of books of the class under treatment,[3] and those descriptive phrases which though they add to the significance of the title do not give enough information to pay for their retention.[4]

[1] *Ex.,* a (plain) treatise on; an (exact and full) account.

[2] In "Compendious pocket dictionary," either compendious or pocket is superfluous.

[3] *Ex.* Nekrolog, 1790–1800 (enthaltend Nachrichten von dem Leben merkwürdiger in diesem Jahre verstorbenen Personen).

[4] "by an American not by birth but by the love of liberty."

113. Omit all other unnecessary words.

In the following examples I use the double (( )) to indicate what every catalogue ought to omit, the single ( ) to indicate what may well be omitted.

Ed. alt. (priore emendatior).

2e éd. (augmentée).

2d ed. (with additions and improvements).

with ((an appendix containing)) problems.

((a collection of)) papers relating to the war in India.

((a series of)) letters.

((On the)) brick architecture of the north of Italy.

(debate) on ((the subject of)) the impressment bill.

on ((the question of)) a financial agent.

((being some)) account of his travels.

in ((the year)) 1875.

Sermons ((on various subjects)). *N. B.* Must occasionally be retained to distinguish different collections of sermons by the same author.

The grounds of infant damnation ((considered in)) (a) sermon ((preached)) Nov. 5, (1717). Boston, 1717. 8°.

Sermon (the Lord's day after the) interment of.

Opera ((quæ extant)) (omnia).

Geology ((of the State)) of Maine.

Tables for ((the use of)) civil engineers.

Reflections ((suggested by a perusal of))* J. H. Palmer's ((pamphlet on the)) "Causes (and consequences) of the war."

Occasioned by his ((book entitled)) "True narrative."

defended against ((the cavils of)) G. Martin.

Howe during his command (of the King's troops) in North America.

So a "Discourse in Albany, Feb. 27, 1848, occasioned by the death of John Quincy Adams, etc. Albany, 1848. 8°," would become Disc., Albany, Feb. 27, death of J. Q. Adams. Albany, 1848. 8°, in Medium, and Short would probably omit "Albany, Feb. 27."

114. For chronological phrases use dates.

Ex. For "from the accession of Edward III. to the death of Henry VIII.," say [1327–1547].

115. In Short and Medium use initials for all Christian names introduced in titles, notes, and contents, and omit the initials altogether for famous men unless there are two of the same name.

Ex. Write "Life of L. V. Bell," "ed. by F. J. Furnivall," but "Lives of Cicero, Milton, Tell, Washington;" and distinguish by initials the Bachs, Grimms, Humboldts, Schlegels. Short may as well omit the initials of editors, translators, etc.

E. g., **Dante.** Divine comedy; tr. by Cayley. London, 1851–54. 4 v. 16°.
— *Same.* Tr. by Wright. London, *Bohn*, 1854. 8°.
— *Same.* Tr. by Longfellow. Boston, 1867. 3 v. 8°.

116. Abbreviate certain common words always, and less common words in a long title which cannot be shortened in any other way.

Abbreviations should suggest the word for which they are used, and should not, if it can be avoided, suggest any other. When one abbreviation is used for two words, if the context does not determine the sense the abbreviation must be lengthened. The most common and useful are Abp. (Archbishop), a. d. Lat. (aus dem Lateinischen), add. (additions), Amer. or Am.

* Substitute [on].

(American), anon. (anonymous), app. (appendix), Aufl., Ausg., or even A. (Auflage, Ausgabe), bibl. (biblical, bibliographical, bibliotheca, &c.), biog. (biographical, biography), Bp. (Bishop), B. S. L., &c. (Bohn's scientific library, &c.), Chr. (Christian), class. (classical), col. or coll. (collections, college), com. (commerce, committee), comp. (compiled, compiler), conc. (concerning), dept. (department), dom. (domestic), ed. (edited, edition, editor), encyc. (encyclopædia), ff. (folios or leaves), geog., geol., geom. (geology, geography, geometry), ges. (gesammelte), Ges. or Gesch. (Geschichte), Gr. (Great, Greek), H. F. L., (Harper's family library), hrsg. (herausgegeben), imp. (imperfect), incl. (including), int. (intorno), lib. (library), mem. (memoir), mis. or miscel. (miscellaneous), nat. (natural), n. d. (no date of publication), n. p. (no place), n. s. (new series), n. t.-p. (no title-page), nouv. (nouvelle), obl. (oblong), p., pp. (page, pages), pseud. (pseudonym, pseudonymous), pt. (part), pub. (published), rec. (recensuit), rel. (relating, relative), rept. (report), rev. (review, revised), s. or ser. (series), sämm. (sämmtlich), sm. (small), soc. (society), t.-p. mut., t.-p. w. (title-page mutilated, wanting), tr. (translated, traduit, tradotto, etc.), trans. (transactions), u. (und), übers. (übersetzt), v. (volume), v. (von, but give van in full), w. (wanting). For others see the lists in various dictionaries and cyclopædias.

117. Express numbers by Arabic figures instead of words.

Ex. With 30000 (not thirty thousand) men; but Charles II., not King Charles the Second.

118. In Short omit all that can be expressed by position.

Ex. In a title-entry

How to observe; by H. Martineau.......... 9287

and in a subject-entry

Horse. CARVER, J. Age of the. Phila., 1818. 12° 9077
MURRAY, W. H. The perfect. Bost., 1873. 8°.......... 1694

If this is thought too disagreeable, use an initial for the heading when it is repeated in the title; as:

Horse. CARVER, J. Age of the H. Phila., 1818. 12° 9077
MURRAY, W. H. The perfect H. Bost., 1873. 8° 1694
SIMPSON, H. H. portraiture. N. Y., 1868. 12° 7407

119. In cataloguing different editions of a book avoid the repetition of the title by using "*Same*."

Ex. **Chaucer,** G. Canterbury tales; [ed.] by T. Tyrwhitt. London, 1822. 5 v. 8°.
— *Same.* Ed. by T. Wright. London, 1847–51. 3 v. 8°.

The word following *Same* should generally begin with a capital.

120. Retain under the author only what is necessary to distinguish the work from other works of the same writer, but under the subject what is needed to state the subject and show how it is treated.

The preface of an excellent catalogue remarks that "the primary object of subject-entries is to inform the reader *who* have written upon a given topic rather than *what* has been written." This is a mistake. The inquirer wishes to know both; in fact he wants to know who have written about it because their character will suggest to him what they have written.

121. Retain both of alternative titles.

Ex. Knights and Sea-Kings; or, The Middle Ages.

The reason is the book may be referred to by either title.

122. Retain in the author-entry the first words of the title; let the abridgement be made farther on.

Because (1) it facilitates library work, by rendering the identification of the book quicker and surer; (2) if there is no part of the title which must be given, two persons may abridge so differently that not a single word shall be the same in the two abridged titles, so that two works will be made out of one (I have often known this to happen); (3) books are frequently referred to by the first word of the title (Grassi's "Notizie sullo stato presente degli Stati

Uniti" may be quoted as Grassi: Notizie). Short, however, can probably not afford to retain first words in all cases. Half the phrases used at the beginning of titles add little or nothing to the meaning, such as "Treatise on," "System of," "Series of lectures on," "Practical hints on the quantitative pronunciation of Latin" (here "Practical hints" belongs in the preface, not in the title, to which it really adds nothing whatever). "History of" must often be retained under the subject. One can say

YOUNG, *Sir* W. Athens. 3d ed. London, 1804;

but under *Athens* that would not be enough; it would be necessary to write

YOUNG, *Sir* W. History of Athens,

to distinguish it from such works as Stuart's "Antiquities of Athens" and Leake's "Topography of Athens." But if there are enough titles under Athens to admit of the subheadings *Art, Antiquities, History,* the words "History of" again become unnecessary. Medium ought always to retain first words under author, and *may* omit them under subject; but such phrases as "Manual of," "Lectures on," do much to explain the character of the book, and for that reason ought often to be retained.

Mottoes, however, at the top of the title-page, separated by a line from the real title, may be neglected. Sometimes such superscriptions are important, generally not.

123. Do not by abridgement render the words retained false or meaningless or ungrammatical.

124. In analyticals, if there are several entries under the author referred to give the first word or words of the title referred to, so that the entry can easily be found; if there are few entries take one or two words which unmistakably identify the book.

A word or two is enough[1] and those abbreviated if possible;[2] but sometimes, when the article has an insufficient or no title it is well to give more of the title of the book in which it is contained, if that is more communicative; *e. g.*, **Wordsworth,** J. Grammatical introduction. (*In his* Fragments of early Latin. 1874.), where "of early Latin" explains "grammatical introduction," and the date shows that the treatise probably embodies the latest ideas.

[1] (*In* **Mueller,** F. M. Chips, v. 1. 1867.) *not* (*In* **Mueller,** F. M. Chips from a German workshop, v. 1. 1867.)

[2] (*In* **Græevius.** Thes. Rom. antiq., v. 10. 1699.)

125. The title is to be copied, so far as it is copied, exactly. Omissions may be made without giving notice to the reader, unless by *etc.* when the sentence is manifestly unfinished.[1] Additions made to a title are to be marked by inclosing the words in brackets [ ].[2] All additions to be in the language of the title; if this cannot be done, put the addition into a note.[3] After a word spelled unusually insert [*sic*].

[1] The use of ... is suited only to bibliographies. I do not see why even Full should use this sign, except for very rare or typographically-important books. The title in a catalogue is not intended to be a substitute for the book itself and must leave some questions to be answered by the latter.

[2] The use of [ ] is important, both as a check on indiscriminate addition and as an aid to identification. It will not often be of use in the latter respect, but as one can never tell when it will be needed it must be employed always.

[3] The intercalation of English words in a foreign title is extremely awkward.

126. State in what language the book is written unless it is evident from the title.

Ex. **Aelianus.** De natura animalium [Gr. et Lat.].

Aeschines. Orations on the crown [Gr.], with Eng. notes.

127. Retain in or add to the title of a translation words stating from what language it was made, unless that is evident from the author's name or is shown by its position after the original title.

Ex. **Beckford,** Wm. Vathek; [tr. fr. the French].
Lessing, Gotthold Ephraim. Laocoon; tr. by E. Frothingham.
Euripides. Ἱππόλυτος στεφανηφόρος.
— *Eng.* The crowned Hippolytus; tr. by M. P. Fitz-Gerald.

128. In the entry of translations after the original give the translated title.

This is for the good of persons unacquainted with the original language, who would not know the book by the foreign title, and also to identify the book, different translations not always having the same title.

Dudevant, Mme. Le château des désertes.
— *Eng.* The castle in the wilderness.
— L'homme de neige.
— *Eng.* The snow man.
Dante. Divina commedia.
— *Eng.* Vision of hell, purgatory, and paradise; tr. by Cary.
— — Divine comedy; tr. by Cayley.

129. In anonymous titles entered under the first word put the transposed article after the first phrase.

Âme en peine, Une, *not* **Âme,** Une, en peine.

130. Under the author distinguish the titles of anonymous books.

Enclosing the dash in brackets is ugly [—]; enclosing the title in brackets is misleading, as if the title were false. Stars (*) or daggers (†) are sometimes prefixed to the title, but they are often used for other purposes and they throw the titles out of line. [*Anon.*] may be used between the title and the imprint; † in the same position would take less room and as soon as accepted would be equally intelligible; it has occasionally been used.

131. In the title-entry of an anonymous work insert the author's name in brackets.

Ex. **Colloquies** of Edw. Osborne; [by M. A. Manning]. London, 1830. 16°.

132. Words like Lord, Gen., Rev., King, ed., tr., occurring in the title are not to be italicized.

133. When the title is in an alphabet which differs from the English, transliterate the first few words and add a translation.

Ex. [Pisni Russkaho naroda; Songs of the Russian people.]

When the title is in Greek followed by a Latin translation it is customary to use the latter alone, and the same may be done in the case of other languages. But for identification it is necessary that some part of the book's own title should be printed. It is not enough to give merely a made title or a translation.

C. Editions.

134. Distinguish editions by the number, the name of the editor, translator, etc., and by mentioning in parentheses (not brackets) after the imprint the collection, library, series, to which it belongs, or the name of the society by which it is published.

Ex. 4th ed., 10th thous., New ed., ed. by T. Good, (Bohn's standard library), (Weale's series, v. 20), (Camden Soc., v. 3). It is shorter and nearly as useful to give Bohn, Weale, etc., as publishers in the imprint,— London, *Bohn,* 1867. 8°.

The various editions of different volumes may be stated thus:

Hales, Stephen. Statical essays. (Vol. 1, 3d ed.) London, 1738, 33. 2 v. 8°.

The specification of edition is necessary: (1) for the student, who often wants a particular edition and cares no more for another than he would for an entirely different work; (2) in the library service, to prevent the rejection of works which are not really duplicates. And the number of the edition is a fact in the literary history of the author worth preserving under his name; under the subject it is some guarantee for the repute, if not for the value, of the work.

135. Full will note carefully whether there is any change in a new edition, or whether it is merely what the Germans call a title-edition (the same matter with a new title-page). Medium and Short generally content themselves with noting the number of the edition. Short often takes no notice of the edition.

D. Imprints.

136. The imprint consists of place of publication, publisher's name, date, number of volumes, typographic form, number of pages, and number of maps, engravings, and the like, which are to be given in the above order.

Washington, 1875. 2 v. 8°, pp. vii, 441, (12); iv, 424; 20 engr., 24 photographs, 4 maps.

The imprint proper consists merely of place, date, form, and number of volumes (Wash., 1875. 2 v. 8°). The other details are given by Medium in particular cases. Full gives them always, but it may be doubted whether their use is frequent enough to pay for the very considerable increase in the trouble of cataloguing. It is worth while to show by some sign (as *p.*) that the pages are less than 100 or than 50 (40 is the limit of the French Bibliothèque Nationale), for the fact is easily ascertained, and the mark fills little space and may prevent some one sending for a book he does not care to look at. It is not an exact designation, but many things are useful which are not exact. On the other hand an inquirer might occasionally fail to see the best treatise on his subject, thinking it too short to be of any value. Neither Short nor Medium should give the exact number of maps, plates, etc., but it is well worth while, especially for a popular library, to add the word *illus.* to the titles of books in which the illustrations are at all prominent, and, under **Biography**, to note the presence of portraits.

Imprints are indispensable in a catalogue designed for scholars, that is for college libraries, for historical or scientific libraries, and for large city libraries. They may not be of much use to nine persons in ten who use those libraries, but they should be inserted for the tenth person. But in the majority of popular city and town libraries neither the character of the readers nor of the books justifies their insertion. Their place may be much better filled (as in the Quincy catalogue) with more important matter — with "*Illus.*" or "*Portraits,*" or a word or two explaining an obscure title. But the number of volumes should invariably be given.

137. Do not translate the name of the place of publication, but if it is not in a Roman alphabet transliterate it.

Göttingen, not Gottingen; München, not Munich; Wien, not Vienna; Londini, not London; Lisboa, not Lisbon, when the first are the forms on the title-page. So [Moskva], Moskau, Moscou, Moscow, according as the imprint is in Russian, German, French, or English.

138. Use abbreviations and even initials for names of the most common places of publication.

Ex. Balt., Berl., Bost., Camb., Cin., Cop. or Copenh., Göt., L. (London), Lisb., Lpz., Madr., N. O., N. Y., Oxf, P. (Paris), Phila., St. P. (St. Petersburg), Ven., Wash.; and use the ordinary abbreviations for state names.

139. If there is more than one place of publication Short and Medium should give only one.

If the places are connected by "and," as London and Edinburgh, New York and London, take the first; if they are unconnected, as

Berlin Paris Genève
H. Baillière

take that which proves on examination to be the real place of publication. In this economy there is some danger of cataloguing the same book at different times with different imprints, and making two editions out of one; but a little watchfulness will prevent this.

140. If the place differs in the different volumes, state the fact.

Ex. — History of England. Vol. 1-2, Boston; 3-5, N. Y., 1867-69. 5 v. 8°.

141. Print publishers' names, when it is necessary to give them, in italics after the place.

Ex. London, *Pickering,* 1849; Antwerpen, *bi mi Claes dic Graue.* The publisher's name must not be mistaken for the place. I have seen a dozen books catalogued as Redfield, 185-. 12°; Redfield being a New York publisher who had a fancy for making his name the most prominent object in the imprint of his books.

142. If the place or date given at the end of the book differs from that on the title-page, or if place and date are given there only, they should be printed in brackets.

Ex. Augsb., 1525 [*colophon* Nuremb., 1526].
Lpz., [*col.* 1571].

143. In early works the date is sometimes given without the century, as "im vierten Jahre," *i. e.*, 1604. Of course the century should be supplied in brackets.

144. Masonic dates should be followed by the date in the usual form.

Ex. 5834 [1834]. 8°.

145. Chronograms should be interpreted and given in Arabic numerals.

Ex. Me DuCit ChrIstVs = 1704.

146. When the place or date is given falsely, whether intentionally or by a typographical error, add the true date in brackets, if it can be ascertained.

Ex. London, 1975 [1775]. 8°.
Paris, 1884 [mistake for 1874]. 8°.

147. When the place or date is not given, supply it in brackets if it can be ascertained. If neither is discoverable, write *n. p.* (= no place), *n. d.* (= no date), to show that the omission of place and date is not an oversight.

Ex. London, *n. p., n. d.* 8°.

148. But avoid *n. d.*, and if possible give the decade or at least the century, even if an interrogation point must be added.

Ex. London, [17—]. 4°.
Phila., [182-?]. 8°.

149. Print the date in Arabic numerals.

Ex. 1517 for M D XVII or CIↃ IↃ XIIIX.

When the subarrangment of the catalogue is by dates (as in that of the Amer. Philos. Society), it may be well to place the date uniformly at the end of the line in this order: 8°. Wash., 1864.

Otherwise the best order is to put the place and date immediately after the title, because like it they are taken from the title-page. The form, which is not copied but is the cataloguer's own assertion, then comes last. The dates can be made prominent in a chronological arrangement by printing them in heavy type, as in Prof. Abbot's "Literature of the doctrine of a future life." In Very Short the German style of printing dates should be adopted, 742 (*i. e.*, 1742), 875 (*i. e.*, 1875).

150. When different volumes of a work were published at different times give the extreme dates.

Ex. Paris, 1840–42. 8°. Sometimes Vol. 1 is of the 2d ed. and its date is later than that of Vol. 2. This is in Medium: (Vol. 1, 2d ed.) 1874, 69–73. 5 v. 8°; in Short merely 1869–74.

151. In cataloguing reprints Full should give the date of the original edition.

Ex. **Ascham,** R. Toxophilus, 1545. London, 1870. 8° (Arber's reprints).
or 3d ed. London, 1857 [1st ed. 1542]. 8°.

The labor of always hunting up the original date is so great that Medium may be allowed to give it when it can easily be ascertained and omit it in other cases.

In a printed catalogue if the first edition is in the library of course its date need not be given with the subsequent editions.

152. In analyticals Medium and Full should give the date of the work referred to, and the number of pages; Short should specify at least which volume is meant.

The date, if it be that of original publication, tends to show the style of treatment; if it be that of a reprint or of "Works" it shows which of the various editions in the library is meant. The number of pages will help the reader to decide whether the reference is worth looking up.

The Birmingham Free Library has an ingenious way of printing analyticals. The title is in long primer type, the parenthesis is in pearl, of which two lines will justify with one of the long primer.

Fossils. Recent and fossil shells by Woodward (Weale's Series, vol. 27.)
Gleig, G. R. Eminent military commanders (Lardner's Cyclopædia, vols. 19-21.) 3 duo 1832.

By this arrangement the analytical nature of the reference is made much clearer and often a line is saved. But it is very troublesome to the printer.

153. Give the number of volumes.

An imperfect set can be catalogued thus:

Vol. 2–4, 6–7. Bost., 1830. 5 v. 8°, *or*
Bost., 1830. 7 v. (v. 5 w.). 8°.

7 v. 8° means Vol. 1–7 if nothing is said to the contrary, and any number of missing volumes can be enumerated in the second of these forms; but as the first volumes of periodicals are often missing, the exception may be made of always cataloguing them in the 1st form. Whatever Short may be forced to do by its system of charging books, Medium and Full ought to give the number of volumes bibliographically, that is to say, they should count only that a volume which has its own title, paging, and register. If the parts of a work have a continuous register or a continuous paging they form one volume; but if they are called Vol. 1, Vol. 2 on the title-page they may be described as 1 v. in 2. For the bibliographical cataloguer binding has nothing to do with the matter. That the binder has joined two or more thin volumes or divided a thick one ought to be recorded in the accessions-book and in the shelf-list, but is not worth notice in the catalogue; if mentioned at all it should be in such a way that the description of the accidental condition of a single copy in a particular library shall not be mistaken for an assertion applicable to a whole edition (thus, 1 v. bd. in 2, or 2 v. bd. in 1, as the case may be). A work which has a title-page (whether or not it has an independent paging or register) but is included in the title-page of another work, is said to be *appended* to that work.

154. Let the form (f°, 4°, 8°, &c.) represent the fold of the sheet as ascertained from the signature, not be guessed from the size.

In the older books this is important, and in modern books the distinction between the octavo and the duodecimo series is so easily ascertained that it is not worth while to be inaccurate. The size may be more exactly indicated, if it is thought worth while, by L. or sm., sq., obl., prefixed to the fold, as L. 8°, sm. 4°. The "vo" or "mo" should be represented by a superior ° if it can be had, otherwise a degree-mark °, though manifestly improper, must be employed; it has abundant usage in its favor.

Another method of giving the form is f° (8), 4° (2), 8° (4), in which f°, 4°, 8° indicate the apparent form of the book as the terms folio, quarto, octavo are generally understood, and the figures within the parentheses show the number of leaves intervening between the successive signatures.

"In the folio the sheet of paper makes two leaves or four pages, in the 4° four leaves, in the 8° eight, in the 12° twelve, and so on. When a sheet of paper is folded into six leaves, making what ought to be a 6° book it is called a 12° printed in half sheets, because such printing is always done with half-sized paper, or with half-sheets, so as to give a 12° size. From a very early period it has been universal to distinguish the sheets by different letters called signatures. At present a sheet has A on the first leaf or A1 on the first leaf and A2 on the second, which is enough for the folder's purpose. But in former times the signatures were generally carried on through half the sheet, and sometimes through the whole. Again, in modern times, no sheet ever goes into and forms part of another; that is, no leaf of any one sheet ever lies between two leaves of another. But in the sixteenth century, and even later in Italy, it was common enough to print in quire-fashion, the same letter being used for the whole quire, and the leaves of the quire distinguished as they were successively placed inside of one another by the figures 2, 3, 4, so that a book actually printed in folio might have the signatures of a modern octavo. In exact bibliography such books are sometimes described as 'folio in twos, 'folio in fours.' Rules are given for determining the form of printing by the water-lines of the paper and by the catchwords. It is supposed that the latter are always at the end of the sheet, and also that the water-lines are perpendicular in folio, octavo, and decimo-octavo books, horizontal in quarto and duodecimo. But in the first place a great many old books have catchwords at the bottom of every page, many have none at all; and as to the rule of water-lines, there are exceptions to every case of it."* Nevertheless it is a generally trustworthy rule.

E. Contents and Notes.

155. Give (under the author) a list of the contents of books containing several works by the same author, or works by several authors, or works on several subjects, or a single work on a number of distinct subjects,[1] especially if the collective title does not sufficiently describe them.[2]

[1] As a collection of lives.

[2] Only Full can give the contents of all such works, including the memoirs, transactions, &c., of all the learned societies. And in an analytical catalogue this is much less important. When every separate treatise is entered in its proper places under the names of its author and of its subject, why should it be given again in a long column of fine type which few persons will ever read? Because, if analysis is not complete, contents supplement it; and one who has forgotten author and subject may occasionally recall them by looking over a "*contents;*" and this list is, so far as it goes, a substitute for a classed catalogue in this respect. Moreover the "*contents*" is needed to fully explain the character of the subject-entry (see § 3). In the division *Biography* under countries we have many such titles as "Memoirs of eminent Englishwomen," "British senators," "Political portraits." It is an advantage to the reader, though perhaps neither a great nor a frequent advantage, to be able to find out from the catalogue what Englishwomen and what British senators he shall find described in the books. No catalogue can be considered complete that omits such information.

* De Morgan, altered.

For collected works of any author "*contents*" have been found so useful that even Short often gives them, especially of late, and strange to say, not rarely prints them in the most extravagant style, allowing a line for each item. One may sometimes see a quarter of a page left bare from this cause.

156. When a single work fills several volumes give the contents under the author, provided the division is definite and easily described.

Object, that the inquirer may know which volume he wants; application, chiefly to dictionaries and historical works; method, in general, giving dates and letters of the alphabet, which take little room. It is particularly important also to fully describe in this way very bulky works; Walton's Polyglott is a good example, in consulting which without such a guide one may have to handle ten gigantic folios.

157. Under the subject repeat so much of the contents as is necessary to show how the subject is treated or what part is treated in the different volumes.

This is particularly desirable in works with an insufficiently descriptive title which treat of several subjects, for which under each heading will be given its appropriate part of the contents. For example, Hugo's "Jus civile Antejustinianeum" contains the originals of Antejustinian law, but this does not appear from its title, and if it did, it would be hardly worth while to save a few lines by obliging the reader to turn to **Hugo** to ascertain just what is in the book. On the other hand the contents of Pertz's "Monumenta Germaniæ historica" is so long that only Fullest can afford to give it under Germany as well as under Pertz. In such a case the reader feels it to be more reasonable that he should be referred.

The contents is often more useful under subject-heading than under author; but it is best that there should be one uniform place where it can always be found, and where the whole of it can be found, and that place should be the author-catalogue.

158. Put into notes (in small type) that information which is not given in the title but is required to be given by the plan of the catalogue.

Notes have several objects:

1. To give any information about the author, the form of his name, his pseudonyms, etc., about the different editions or places of publication, or about the gaps in a set (especially of periodicals), which cannot be included in the title without making it disproportionately long. Short, especially if without imprints, can get many of these into the title; which it is well to do, for a short note is not economical.

2. To explain the title or correct any misapprehension to which it might lead. In a popular library the boys take out "The cruise of the Betsy," imagining it to be another "Cruise of the Midge."

3. To direct the attention of persons not familiar with literature to the best books. The main principles of such annotating are simple. (*a.*) The notes should characterize the best books only; to insert them under every author would only confuse and weary; if few they will arrest attention much better. Dull books and morally bad books should be left in obscurity. Under some of the poorer works which have attained unmerited popularity a brief protest may be made; it will probably be ineffectual; but it can do no harm to call Mühlbach unreliable or Tupper commonplace. (*b.*) They should be brief and pointed. Perhaps after this direction it is necessary to add that they should be true.

4. To lay out courses of reading for that numerous class who are desirous of "improving their minds," and are willing to spend considerable effort and time but know neither where to begin nor how to go on.

F. References.

159. In references use the word *See* when there is no entry under the heading from which the reference is made; *See also* when there is one.

Ex. **Death penalty.** *See* **Capital punishment.**
Horticulture. LINDLEY, J. Theory of H.
See also **Flowers; — Fruit.**

Not *Vide;* the language of an English catalogue should be English.

160. References must be brief.

Yet the convenience of the public must not be sacrificed to brevity. If, for instance, several authors had used the same pseudonym, the titles of their respective works should be given in the references that the reader may know under which of the authors he will find the work he is in search of, and not have to turn to all three.

Detlef, Carl, *pseud.* *See* **Baur**, C.

is the usual form of reference; but it is not enough for Hamilton.

Hamilton, *pseud.* Essay on a congress of nations. *See* **Whitman**, G. H.

Hamilton, *pseud.* Hamilton. No. 1, *etc.* *See* **Carey**, M.

Analytical references to treatises of the same author or on the same subject, contained in different volumes of the same work may be made thus:

Charles, A. O. Reformatory and refuge union. (*In* **National Assoc. Prom. Soc. Sci.** Trans., 1860.) — Reformatory legislation. (*In* Trans., 1861.) — Punishment and reformation in America. (*In* Trans., 1863.)

Comets. PEIRCE, B. Connection of comets with the solar system. (*In* **Amer. Assoc.**, Proc., v. 2. 1850.) — HUBBARD, J. S. Biela's double comet. (*In* v. 8.) — KIRKWOOD, D. Mean distances of the periodic comet. (*In* v. 12. 1859.)

G. CAPITALS.

161. In English use an initial capital

1. for the first word
   a. of every sentence.
   b. of every title quoted.
   c. of every alternative title.
2. for all proper names
   a. of persons and places,
   b. of bodies,
   c. of noted events and periods,
   } each separate word not an article or preposition.

N. B. This does not include names of genera, species, etc., in the animal and vegetable kingdoms, which in an ordinary catalogue should not be capitalized; as digitalis purpurea, raia, batis, the horse.

3. for titles of honor.

Ex. 1 *b.* Reply to the Essay on the discovery of America.
1 *c.* Institutio legalis; or, Introduction to the laws of England. But it is better, when the sense will permit, to omit the "or" and consider the second title as a clause explanatory of the first, as Institutio legalis; introduction to the laws of England.
2 *b.* Society for Promoting the Diffusion of Useful Knowledge.
2 *c.* Boston Massacre, French Revolution, Gunpowder Plot, Middle Ages.
3. King, Earl, Gen., Capt., Rev., etc.

162. In foreign languages use initial capitals

4. for 1 *a*, 1 *b*, 1 *c*.
5. (Persons and places) *a.* In *German* and *Danish* for every noun and for adjectives derived from names of persons, but for no others.
   b. in the *Romance* languages (*Italian*, *French*, *Spanish*, *Portuguese*) and in *Swedish* and *Greek* for proper names of persons and places, but not for adjectives derived from them.

c. in *Latin* and *Dutch* for proper names and also for the adjectives derived from them, but not for common nouns.

6. (Bodies) as in English, except that in *German* and *Danish* only the nouns are to be capitalized, and adjectives when they begin the name.
7. (Events and periods) as in English, with the same exception.
8. (Titles) in *German* and *Danish*, but not in the *Romance* languages, in *Latin* or in *Greek*.

Ex. 5 *a.* Die Homerische Frage, but Die griechischen Scholien. In many German books capitals are not used even for adjectives derived from personal names.

5 *b.* Les Français, but le peuple français.

6. Société de l'Histoire de France.

7. Le Moyen Âge, la Révolution Française, Die französische Revolution. The French, however, now generally print le moyen âge, la révolution française. Capitals are to be avoided, because in the short sentences of which a catalogue consists they confuse rather than help the eye. For this reason it is better not to capitalize names in natural history whether English or Latin (bee, rana pipiens, liliaceæ, etc.). Several libraries following the lead of the Congress catalogue have discarded capitals for German nouns. Grimm's authority is alleged in justification, but Grimm's example is followed by a very small minority even of German scholars, and the titles so printed still have an awkward look to most readers. One might as well follow Furnivall and the Early English Text Society in askt, catalogd. The Boston Public Library also goes to an extreme in its avoidance of capitals, not using them for such proper names as methodists, protestant episcopal church, royal society, etc.

The names of languages are not to be capitalized in the Romance languages, as "traduit de l'anglais," "in francese."

Titles of honor are not to be capitalized in the Romance languages, as *comte, roi, conte, marchese.* But *Monsieur, Madame, Signor, Don, Donna* always begin with capitals.

It is probably most common to use capitals for the numbers after the names of kings (as Charles III.) and for the abbreviations A.D., B C. Small capitals, however, are more pleasing, as, "The life of Tiberius, extending from B.C. 42 to A.D. 14, was filled, etc."

H. Punctuation, etc.

163. Let each entry consist of four (or five) sentences:

1. the heading,	**Cicero,** Marcus Tullius.
2. the title, including editors and translators,	Brutus de claris oratoribus; erkl. von O. Jahn.
3. the edition,	2e Aufl.
4. the imprint, as given by the book,	Berlin, 1856.
5. the part of the imprint added by the cataloguer,	8°.

Which, if not the first title under Cicero, would read:

— Brutus de claris oratoribus; erkl. von O. Jahn. 2e Aufl. Berlin, 1856. 8°.

This requires a minimum of capitals. It will occasionally happen that the title cannot be thrown into one sentence, but it should always be done when possible. It is usual to separate 4 and 5. The French however make one sentence of them (Paris, 1864, in-12). This has the advantage of agreeing with the best form of quoting a title ("see his Memoirs, London, 1874, 8°, in which," &c.). It is useless for one who abridges titles to make any attempt to follow the punctuation. The spelling should be retained, but it is hardly worth while for Short or Medium to imitate the old printers in their indiscriminate use of i and j, u and v.

A library may have a collection of books or a few volumes which from their rarity deserve to be catalogued with every bibliographical nicety, with the most exact copying of punctuation, spelling, and forms of letters, and even with marks to show where the lines of the title end. Such collections are the Prince and the Ticknor books in the Boston Public Library, such single books are fifteeners or the rarest Americana. Yet it may be questioned whether a library does well to redescribe books already fully described by Hain, Harrisse, Thiele, Trömmel, Stevens, or Sabin. A simple reference to these works will generally suffice (§ 205).

164. Supply the proper accents if they are not given in the title.

In French and Greek titles printed in capitals the accents are often omitted. In the titles of rare books, copied exactly, accents should not be supplied.

165. Use [ ] only for words added to the title, and ( ) to express inclusion.

Ex. **Talbot**, E. A. Five years residence in Canada, [1818–23].

Maguire, J. F. Canada. (*In his* Irish in America. 1868.)

Bale, J. Kinge John, a play; ed. by J. P. Collier. Westm., 1838. 4°. (Camden Soc., v. 2.)

166. If any title contains [ ] or ( ) omit them, using commas instead.

One sign should never be used to express two things if that can be avoided; each should have one definite meaning.

167. Use italics for the words *See* or *See also* in references, *In* and *In his* in analyticals, and for *Note*, *Contents*, and *Namely*, also for subdivisions of subjects.

168. In long *Contents* make the division of the volumes plain either by heavy-faced volume-numbers or by giving each volume a separate paragraph.

Anyone will recoil from the labor of looking through a long undivided mass of small type; moreover the reader ought to be able to determine at once in what volume any article whose title he is reading is contained.

I. Arrangement.

169. Arrange entries according to the English alphabet, whatever the order of the alphabet in which a foreign name might have to be entered in its original language.

Treat **I** and **J**, **U** and **V**, as separate letters; **ij**, at least in the older Dutch names, should be arranged as **y**; do not put Spanish names beginning with **Ch**, **Ll**, **Ñ**, after all other names beginning with **C**, **L**, and **N**, as is done by the Spanish Academy.

1. Headings.

170. When the same word serves for several kinds of heading let the order be the following: person, place, title, subject (except person or place), form.

Arrangement must be arbitrary. This order is easy to remember because it follows the course of cataloguing; we put down first the author, then the title, and lastly look inside for the subject. Of course, the person considered as a subject cannot be separated from the person as author. As the place may be either author or subject or both, it may come between the two.

Ex. **Washington**, George. (person)

Washington, *D. C.* (place)

Homes, H. A. (person)

Homes family. (persons)

Homes and shrines. (title)

Homes. (subject).

171. Christian names used as headings precede surnames.

Ex. **Christian** II.
Christian, James.
Christian art.
Francis II.
Francis, Abraham.
Francis and Jane.

172. Headings like Charles, George, Henry, when very numerous, must be divided into classes, in this order: Saints, Popes, Emperors, Kings, Princes and Noblemen, others; and the names of each class arranged in alphabetical order of countries, and under countries arranged numerically.

Ex. **Peter**, *Saint.*
Peter, *Pope.*
Peter *the Great, Emperor of Russia.*
Peter II. *of Aragon.*
Peter III. *of Aragon.*
Peter I. *of Portugal.*
Peter, *Duke of Newcastle.*
Peter, *of Groningen, enthusiast. See* **Pieter.**
Peter, John Henry.
Peter, Lake.
Peter, Mt.
Peter Lewis, a true tale.
Peter-Hansen, Erik.

173. Arrange proper names beginning with **M', Mc, St., Ste.**, as if spelled **Mac, Saint, Sainte.**

Because they are so pronounced. But L' is not arranged as La or Le, nor O' as if it stood for Of, because they are not so pronounced.

174. Arrange by the Christian name headings in which the family name is the same.

No attention is to be paid to the titles *Sir, Mrs., Capt.*, &c. In regard to *Hungarian* names observe that the name appears on the title-page as it does in a catalogue, the family name first, followed by the Christian name; as "Elbeszélések; irta báró **Eötvös** Jozsef.

175. When the Christian names are the same arrange chronologically.

Again no attention is to be paid to the titles *Sir*, etc. The alphabetical principle is of no use here because no one can know beforehand which of many possible titles we have taken to arrange by, whereas some one may know when the author whom he is seeking lived. Of course

Brown, T. L., comes before
Brown, Thomas, for the same reason that
Brown comes before
Browne.

Christian names not generally used should be spaced or parenthesized, because when there are several this assists the eye in picking out the right one. Thus if we have

Franklin, John, *d.* 1759,
Franklin, *Sir* John, *d.* 1863,
Franklin, John Andrew,
Franklin, John Charles,
Franklin, John D a v i d,

the reader not knowing of the name David would expect to find the last among the simple Johns, but seeing the David spaced would understand that it was a rarely used name. This supposes that he knows the system, but one cannot have a condensed catalogue without obliging the reader to learn how to use it.

176. Arrange a nobleman's title or the name of a bishop's see, from which reference is made to the family name, among the personal names, not with the places.

Ex. **London**, Alfred.
London, David, *Bp. of*
London, John.
London, *Conn.*
London, *Eng.*
not **London**, John.
London, David, *Bp. of*
London, *Conn.*
nor **London**, John.
London, *Conn.*
London, David, *Bp. of*
London, *Eng.*

Danby, John.
Danby, Thomas, *Earl of*
Danby, Wm.
Danby, *Eng.*

177. The possessive case singular should be arranged with the plural.

The alphabet demands this and I see no reason to make an exception which cannot be made in foreign languages.

Bride of Lammermoor.
Brides and bridals.
Bride's choice.

178. Arrange Greek and Latin personal names by their patronymics or other appellatives.

Ex. **Dionysius.**
Dionysius *Areopagita.*
Dionysius *Chalcidensis.*
Dionysius *Genuensis.*

179. Arrange English personal names compounded with *prefixes* as single words; also those foreign names in which the prefix is not transposed (see § 17).

Ex. **Demonstration.**
De Montfort.
Demophilus.
De Morgan.
Demosthenes.

Other such names are Ap Thomas, Des Barres, Du Chaillu, Fitz Allen, La Motte Fouqué, Le Sage, Mac Fingal, O'Neal, Saint-Réal, Sainte-Beuve, Van Buren.

This is the universal custom, founded on the fact that the prefixes are often not separated in printing from the following part of the name. It would of course be wrong to have **Demorgan** in one place and **De Morgan** in another.

180. Arrange personal names compounded of *two names* after the first name but before the next longer word.

Ex. **Fonte**, Bart. de.
Fonte Resbecq, Auguste.
Fontenay, Louis.
Fontenay Mareuil, François.

181. Arrange compound names of *places* as separate words.

Ex. **New**, John.
New Hampshire.
New legion of Satan.
New Sydenham Society.
New York.
Newark.
Newfoundland.
Newspapers.

not **New**, John.
New legion of Satan.
Newark.
Newfoundland.
New Hampshire.
Newspapers.
New Sydenham Society.
New York.

182. Arrange names of *societies* as separate words.

See **New Sydenham Society** in the list above.

183. Arrange *hyphened* words as if separate.

Ex. **Happy** home.
Happy-Thought Hall.
Happy thoughts.
Sing, *pseud.*
Sing, James.
Sing, James, *pseud.*
Sing-Sing Prison.
Sing-Song melodies.
Singapore.
Singing.

Grave and Reverend Club.
Grave County.
Grave Creek.
Grave-mounds.
Grave objections.
Grave de Mézeray, Antoine.
Gravel.
Graves.
Out and about.
Out-of-door Parliament.
Out in the cold, a song.

184. Arrange *pseudonyms* after the corresponding real name.

Andrew, *pseud.*
Andrew, *St.*
Andrew, *St.*, *pseud.*
Andrew, John.
Andrew, John, *pseud.*
Andrew, John Albion.

185. Arrange abbreviations as if spelled in full.

Ex. Dr., M., Mlle., Mme., Mr., Mrs., as Doctor, Monsieur, etc.

☞ The arrangement recommended in §§ 179–183 suits the eye best and requires as little knowledge or thought as any to use. The exception made in § 179 is required by universal practice and by the fact that a very large part of the personal names beginning with prefixes are commonly printed as one word. Names of places beginning with New, Old, Red, Blue, Green, &c. (which might be likened to the prefixes De, Des, Du, &c., and made the ground of a similar exception) are much less frequently printed as one, and when they are the accent is different. Moreover the words New, Old, etc., have an independent meaning and occur as personal names, first-words of titles, or of the names of societies, as in the examples in § 181. The reason for separating New Hampshire and Newark in the first example is patent to every consulter at a glance; the reason for the different positions of New legion and New York in the second example would not be clear and would have to be thought out; and it is not well to demand thought from those who use the catalogue if it can be avoided.

2. Titles.

186. Under an author's name adopt the following order: (1) Complete (or nearly complete) works, (2) Smaller collections, (3) Single works, (4) Works written in conjunction with others, (5) Works about him.

Nos. 1–4 come first as belonging to the author-catalogue; 5 comes last as belonging to the subject-catalogue.

Occasionally it is better to let the smaller collections come in their alphabetical place with the single works. The single works of a voluminous author (as Aristotle, Cicero, Homer, Shakespeare) should be so printed that the different titles will strike the eye readily. If the *"contents"* of the collected works are not printed alphabetically, it is well to insert under the titles of the chief single works a reference to the particular volumes of the collections in which they are to be found. (See Boston Athenæum catal., art. **Goethe.**)

If there are only two joint authors let both appear in the heading, and arrange the entry after the works written by the first author alone; if there are more than two make the heading in the form **Smith**, John, *and others*, and arrange the entry under the name of the first author, after the class of entries just mentioned,— works by two authors.[1] If there are two or more combinations, arrange them in the order of the second names.[2]

[1] **Green**, T.
— *and* **White**, S.
— *and others.*

[2] **Brown**, J., *and* **Jones**, R.
— *and* **Robinson**, J.
— *and* **Smith**, J.

187. In the order of titles take account of every word except initial articles.

Address of Southern delegates in Congress.
Address of the people of Great Britain.
Address of twenty thousand loyal Protestant apprentices.
Address on a national education.
Address to a provincial bashaw.
Address to Christians, recommending the distribution.

188. Arrange different editions of the same works chronologically.

Ex. **Homerus.** Carmina [Gr.]; cum annot., cur. C. G. Heyne. Lips., 1802. 8 v. 8°.
— *Same.* [Gr.]; cum notis et proleg. R. P. Knight. Londini, 1820. 4°.
— *Same.* [Gr.]; ed. J. Bekker. Bonnæ, 1858. 2 v. 8°.
Bartlett, John. Collection of familiar quotations. 3d ed. Camb., 1860. 12°.
— *Same.* 4th ed. Boston, 1863. 12°.
— *Same.* 7th ed. Boston, 1875. 16°.

189. Disregard numerals commencing a title before such words as Report, Annual report.

Not		*but*	
	First report,		General account
	Fourth report,		1st, 2d, 4th report.
	General account,		
	Second report.		

190. Arrange translations immediately after the original, prefixing the name of the language into which they are made; if there are several, arrange the languages alphabetically.

Ex. **Cicero.** De officiis. [Various editions, arranged chronologically.]
— *Same.* Erkl. von O. Heine. Berlin, 1857. 8°.
— *Eng.* Offices; tr. by C. R. Edmonds. London, 1850. 8°.
— *French.* Les offices; tr. par [G. Dubois]. Paris, 1691. 8°.

If the original is not in the library the translation may be arranged either by the first words of its own title or by the first words of the original title prefixed in brackets. The latter order is to be preferred when most of the other titles are in the original language. When the list of entries is long a reference should be made from any title of a translation which is alphabetically much separated from its original back to the original title under which it is to be found.

Ex. **Dudevant.** L'homme de neige.
— *Eng.* The snow man.
[58 titles interposed.]
— The snow man. *See, back,* L'homme de neige.

191. Divide the works *about* a person when numerous by collecting the lives into a group.

192. When a writer is voluminous insert the criticisms or notes on or replies to each work after its title; otherwise give them according to § 186, at the end of the article.

193. Arrange analyticals, when there are several for the same article, chronologically, as being different editions.

Ex. **Pretty,** F. Prosperous voyage of Sir T. Cavendish. (*In* **Purchas,** S. Pilgrims, v. 1, b. 2. 1625; — **Harris,** J. Col., v. 1. 1705; *and* v. 1. 1764; — **Callander,** J. Terra Austr., v. 1. 1768; — **Hakluyt,** R. Col., v. 4. 1811.)

194. Under countries arrange titles as under any other author.

That is, put first the country's own works (governmental publications), then the works about the country; and as we put the criticisms on a voluminous author after the separate writings to which they respectively apply, so we put accounts of or attacks upon any branch of government after the entry of the branch.

195. In arranging government publications make all necessary divisions but avoid subdivision.

It is much clearer—and it is the dictionary plan—to make the parts of a division themselves independent divisions, referring from the including division to the subordinate one. *E. g.* (to take part of the headings under **United States**):

Subordination.	*Better order.*
United States. Department of the Interior.	**U. S.** Adjutant General.
Bureau of Indian Affairs.	Bureau of Engineers.
Patent Office.	Bureau of Indian Affairs.
Pension Office.	Bureau of Navigation.
Public Land Office.	Bureau of Navy Yards and Docks.
Department of the Navy.	Bureau of Topographical Engineers.
Bureau of Navigation.	Commissary General.
Hydrographic Office.	Department of the Interior.
Naval Academy.	Department of the Navy.
Naval Observatory.	Department of War.
Bureau of Navy Yards and Docks.	Freedmen's Bureau.
Naval Asylum.	Hydrographic Office.
Department of War.	Military Academy.
Adjutant General's Office.	Naval Academy.
Bureau of Engineers.	Naval Asylum.
Bureau of Topographical Engineers.	Naval Observatory.
Commissary General's Office.	Patent Office.
Freedmen's Bureau.	Pension Office.
Military Academy.	Public Lands.

The subordination of bureaus and offices to departments is adopted simply for convenience and is changed from time to time as the exigencies of the public service demand. There is no corresponding convenience in preserving such an order in a catalogue, but inconvenience, especially in the case of the above-mentioned changes. The alphabetical arrangement has here all its usual advantages without its usual disadvantage of wide separation.

196. Insert a synopsis of the arrangement whenever there are enough titles under a heading to require it.

This applies chiefly to the larger countries (as **France, Great Britain, United States**), the more voluminous authors (as **Cicero, Shakespeare**), one title-entry (**Bible**), and possibly some subjects not national. The arrangement of titles under **Bible** will be governed by §§ 185, 186, 190, and 192; but it can be best understood from an example in some catalogue which has many titles under that heading. The synopsis in the Boston Athenæum catalogue is as follows:

Whole Bibles (first Polyglots then single languages arranged alphabetically).

Works illustrating the whole Bible (under the heads Analysis, Antiquities, Bibliography, Biography, Canon, Catechisms, historical and theological, Commentaries, Concordances, Criticism, Dictionaries, Evidences, authority, etc., Geography, Hermeneutics, History, Inspiration, Introductions, Natural history, Science and the Bible, Theology, morals, etc., Miscellaneous illustrative works).

Selections from both Testaments.
Prophetical books of both Testaments.
Old Testament.
Illustrative works.
Parts of the Old Testament (arranged in the order of the English version), and works severally illustrating them.
Apocrypha.
New Testament.
Illustrative works.
Parts of the New Testament, and works illustrating them.
Under each part the order is: Editions of the original texts chronologically arranged;—Versions, in the alphabetical order of the languages;—Illustrative works.

3. Contents.

197. Arrange *contents* either in the order of the volumes or alphabetically by the titles of the articles.

Alphabetical order.

Contents. Argentile and Curan; a legendary drama, v. 2.
Art of painting, by Du Fresnoy, v. 3.
Caractacus; a dramatic poem, v. 2.
Chronological list of painters to 1689, v. 3.
Dryden's preface to his translation of Du Fresnoy, v. 3.
Elegies, v. 1.
Elfrida; a dramatic poem, v. 2.
English garden, The, v. 1.
Epitaphs and inscriptions, v. 1.
Essay on the meaning of the word angel, as used by St. Paul, v. 4.
Essays on English church music, v. 3.
Examination of the prophecy in Matthew 24th, v. 4.
Hymns and psalms, v. 1.
Musæus, a monody to the memory of Mr. Pope, v. 1.
Odes, v. 1.
Pygmalion, a lyrical scene, v. 2.
Religio clerici, v. 1.
Sappho, a lyrical drama, v. 2.
Sermons, v. 4.
Sonnets, v. 1.

Volume order.

Contents. Vol. **1.** Musæus, a monody to the memory of Mr. Pope.—Odes, sonnets, epitaphs and inscriptions, elegies.—The English garden.—Religio clerici.—Hymns and psalms. **2.** Elfrida, a dramatic poem.—Caractacus, a dramatic poem.—Sappho.—Argentile and Curan, a legendary drama.—Pygmalion, a lyrical scene. **3.** Du Fresnoy's art of painting.—Dryden's preface to his translation of Du Fresnoy.—Chronological list of painters to 1689.—Essays on English church music. **4.** Sermons.—Essay on the meaning of the word angel, as used by St. Paul.—Examination of the prophecy in Matthew 24th.

It is evident how much more compendious the second method is. But there is no reason why an alphabetical "contents" should not be run into a single paragraph.

The titles of novels and plays contained in any collection ought to be entered in the main alphabet; it is difficult then to see the advantage of an alphabetical arrangement of the same titles under the collection. Many other collections are composed of works for which alphabetical order is no gain, because the words of their titles are not mnemonic words, and it is not worth while to take the trouble of arranging them; but there are others composed of both classes, in which such order may be convenient.

4. Subjects.

198. Care must be taken not to mix two subjects together because their names are spelled in the same way.

Thus **Grace** before meals, **Grace** of body, **Grace** the musical term, and **Grace** the theological term, must be four distinct headings.

199. Under subject-headings group titles topically when it can be done, otherwise arrange them by the authors' names.

Alphabetical arrangement by authors' names is useful when a subject-entry is a substitute for a title-entry, but otherwise is as useless as it is inappropriate. If the author's name is known the book should be looked for under that, not under the subject; if it is not known, what good can an arrangement by authors do? Sometimes, if one has forgotten the Christian name of an author, it may be easier to find him under a subject than in a crowd of Smiths or Joneses or Muellers, and this use of a subject-heading is impaired by grouping or by chronological order; but such use is infrequent, and the main design of a subject-entry should not be subordinated to this side advantage.

It is even urged that it is harder to find a work treating of the subject in any special way among subdivisions than when there is only one alphabet, which is absurd. On the one hand one must look over a list of books embracing five or six distinct divisions of a subject and select from titles often ambiguous or provokingly uncommunicative those that seem likely to treat of the matter in the way desired. On the other plan he must run over five or six headings given by another man, and representing that man's ideas of classification, and decide under which of them the treatise he is in search of is likely to be put. Which system gives the least trouble and demands the least brain-work? Plainly the latter. In three cases out of four he can comprehend the system at a glance. And if in the fourth there is a doubt, and he is compelled after all to look over the whole list or several of the divisions, he is no worse off than if there were no divisions; the list is not any longer. The objection then to subdivisions is not real, but fanciful. The reader at first glance is frightened by the appearance of a system to be learned and perversely regards it as a hinderance instead of an assistance. But if anyone has such a rooted aversion to subdivisions it is very easy for him to disregard them altogether, and read the list as if they were not there, leaving them to be of service to wiser men.

As the number of titles under each heading increases in number so does the opportunity and need of division. The first and most usual groups to be made are *Bibliography* and its companion *History* and the "practical-form" groups *Dictionaries* and *Periodicals.* Under countries the first grouping will be *Description and Travels, History and Politics, Language and Literature,* followed by *Natural history,* &c. For examples of further subdivisions see the longer catalogues. It is not worth while in a printed catalogue to make very minute divisions. The object aimed at, — enabling the enquirer to find quickly the book that treats of the branch of the subject which *he* is interested in, — is attained if the mass of titles is broken up into sections containing from half a dozen to a score. Of course there are masses of titles which cannot be so broken up because they all treat of the same subject in the same way, or at least show no difference of treatment that admits of classification. The general works of the Fine Arts in a library of 100,000 volumes may number 100 titles, even after *Periodicals* and *Dictionaries* have been set aside.

There is one objection to grouping, — that books can seldom be made to fill any classification exactly, their contents overrunning the classes, so that they must be entered in several places, or they will fail to be found under some of the subdivisions of which they treat. Thus in the chronological arrangement of *History,* whether we arrange by the first date, the average, or the last date of each work, the books cover periods of such various length that one can never get all that relates to one period together.

There is another objection, — that it is much harder to make a catalogue with subdivisions, which of course require a knowledge of the subject and examination of the books; and the difficulty increases in proportion to the number of the books and the minuteness of the divisions.

200. The subarrangement in groups will often be alphabetical by authors; but in groups or subjects of a historical character it should be chronological.

Thus under countries the division *History* will be arranged according to the period treated of, the earliest first; so under *Description*, for England as seen by foreigners in the days of Elizabeth was a very different country from the England seen by Prince Pueckler-Muskau in 1828, or satirized by Matthew Arnold in 1871. So *Statistics* and *Literature*, and other divisions, should be treated when they are long enough. When there are very few titles, chronological arrangement is confusing, because, unless the order is brought out very clearly by putting the dates first or by printing them in heavy-faced type, it looks as if there was no order at all.

201. When there are many cross-references classify them.

Ex. **Architecture**. *See also* **Arches**;—**Baths**;—**Bridges**;—**Cathedrals**;—**Fonts**;—[and many other things built];
also **Carpentry**;—**Drawing**;—**Metal-work**;—**Painting**;—[and many other means or methods of building];
also **Athens**;—**Berlin**;—**Boston**;—**Milan**;—**Rome**;—**Venice**;—**Verona**;—[and many other cities whose buildings are described];
also **Arabia**;—**Assyria**;—**Egypt**;—**France**;—**Greece**;—**India**;—**Italy**;—[and many other countries whose architecture is described].

202. When the titles are numerous under a subject-heading divide them, but avoid subdivision.

It may not be best to adopt strictly the same method in the subdivisions under countries that was recommended for government publications. There are advantages in both the following plans. The second is the dictionary plan pure and simple; the first is a bit of classification introduced for special reasons into a dictionary catalogue, and perhaps out of place there. It is however the one which I have adopted for the catalogue of the Boston Athenæum.

[Name of country]
Administration.
Agriculture.
Antiquities.
Architecture.
Army.
Art.
Biography.
Botany.
Calendar.
Ceremonies.
Charities.
Climate.
Colonies.
Commerce and Trade.
Costume.
Description and Travels.
Ecclesiastical history.
Education.
Entomology.
Finance.
Folk-lore.
Foreign relations.
Geology.
Heraldry.
Herpetology.

[Name of country.]
Administration.
Agriculture.
Antiquities.
Architecture.
Army.
Art.
Ballads and Songs.
Bibliography.
Botany.
Calendar.
Ceremonies.
Charities.
Climate.
Colonies.
Commerce.
Composition.
Conversation and Phrases.
Correspondence.
Costume.
Description and Travels.
Dialects.
Dialogues.
Dictionaries.
Drama.
Ecclesiastical history.

- History.
  - Bibliography.
  - General works.
  - Chronological arrangement.
- Ichthyology.
- Industry.
- Language.
  - Bibliography.
  - Composition.
  - Conversation and Phrases.
  - Correspondence.
  - Dialects.
  - Dictionaries.
  - Epithets.
  - Etymology.
  - Exercises.
  - General and miscellaneous works.
  - Grammar.
  - Historical grammars.
  - History.
  - Homonyms.
  - Pronunciation and spelling.
  - Prosody.
  - Readers (for foreign languages).
  - Rhymes.
  - Synonyms.
- Law.
  - Bibliography.
  - History.
  - General works.
- Literature.
  - General
    - Bibliography.
    - History (including lives of authors).
    - Collections.
    - Manuals.
    - Selections for reading and speaking.
  - Ballads and songs.
  - Dialogues.
  - Drama.
  - Eloquence or oratory.
  - Epigrams.
  - Epitaphs.
  - Essays.
  - Fables.
  - Fairy tales.
  - Fiction.
  - Legends.
  - Letters.
  - Parodies.
  - Periodicals.
  - Poetical romances.

- Education.
- Eloquence or Oratory.
- Entomology.
- Etymology.
- Epigrams.
- Epitaphs.
- Epithets.
- Exercises.
- Fables.
- Fairy tales.
- Fiction.
- Finance.
- Foreign relations.
- Geology.
- Grammar.
- Heraldry.
- Herpetology.
- History.
  - Bibliography.
  - General works.
  - Chronological arrangement.
- Homonyms.
- Ichthyology.
- Language.
  - Bibliography.
  - History.
  - General and miscellaneous works.
- Law.
  - Bibliography.
  - General works.
  - General and miscellaneous works.
- Legends.
- Letters.
- Literature.
  - Bibliography.
  - History.
  - General and miscellaneous works.
  - Collections.
- Malacology.
- Manufactures.
- Medicine.
- Mineralogy.
- Money.
- Music.
- Names.
- Natural history.
- Navy.
- Naval history.
- Numismatics.
- Ornithology.
- Palæontology.
- Parodies.

Poetry.
Popular literature.*
Prose romances.
Satire.
Sonnets.
Wit and humor.
Malacology.
Manufactures.
Medicine.
Mineralogy.
Money.
Music.
Names.
Natural history.
Navy.
Naval history.
Numismatics.
Ornithology.
Palæontology.
Philosophy.
Politics.
Population.
Public works.
Registers.
Religion.
Sanitary affairs.
Science.
Social distinctions.
Social life, Manners and customs.
Social science.
Statistics.
Technology.
Theatre.
Theology.
Zoölogy.
&c.

Periodicals.
Philosophy.
Poetical romances.
Poetry.
Politics.
Popular literature.*
Population.
Pronunciation.
Prose romances.†
Prosody.
Public works.
Registers.
Religion.
Rhymes.
Sanitary affairs.
Satire.
Science.
Social distinctions.
Social life, Manners and customs.
Social science.
Sonnets.
Spelling.
Statistics.
Synonyms.
Technology.
Theatre.
Theology.
Wit and humor.
Zoölogy.
&c.

Note, however, that if the subordination under Language and Literature is objected to, it is very easy to make them independent headings in the main alphabet, having

instead of		the headings	
Italy.	*Description.*	**Italian language.**	
	History.	**Italian literature.**	
	Language.	**Italy.**	*Description.*
	Literature.		*History.*
	Natural history.		*Natural history.*

Of course different countries will require different divisions, e. g., *Ecclesiastical history, Mythology, Religion, Theology* will not often be required for the same country. And often it will be expedient to combine those divisions in which there are very few titles into one more general; thus *Botany, Herpetology, Ichthyology, Zoölogy* would join to give *Natural history* a respectable size, and *Geology, Mineralogy, Palæontology, Physical geography* would combine, or in very small countries all these would go together under *Description.* Under some countries other divisions will be required; in the list are given only those in actual use; but the arrangement is elastic and admits of new divisions whenever they are needed. In regard to a few (such as *Epitaphs, Fables, Names, Proverbs*) there is room for doubt whether they ought

* Not meaning novels, but broadsides, chap-books, and the like,—the literature of the people in times past.
† Again not meaning novels, but the romances of chivalry, etc.

to be under countries; whether the subject cohesion is not much stronger than the national cohesion. Many others are not usually put here (as *Numismatics, Philosophy, Religion, Science, Theology, Zoölogy*). The former usage was to put under the country only its history, travels in it, and the general descriptive works; and books that treated of the Art, Architecture, Ballads, Botany, Drama, &c., of that land were put with the general works on Art, Architecture, &c. But the tendency of the dictionary catalogue is towards national classification, that is, in separating what relates to the parts of a subject, as is required by its *specific* principle, it necessarily brings together all that relates to a country in every aspect, as it would what relates to any other individual.

It may be asked (1) why the parts of *Natural history* are here separated and the parts of *Language* and *Literature* not; and (2) why we do not divide still more (following out the dictionary plan fully), so as to have divisions like *Liliaceæ, Cows, Horses.* As to (2), in a library catalogue of a million volumes it would no doubt be best to adopt rigidly this specific mode of entry for the larger countries; for a catalogue of one or two hundred thousand, arrangement in classes is as well suited to quick reference and avoids the loss of room occasioned by numerous headings. With few books minute division has a very incomplete appearance, specialties occurring only here and there, and most of the titles being those of general works. This may be compared to the division of a library into alcoves. One of from 10,000 to 20,000 volumes has an alcove for natural history; from 20,000 to 50,000 it has alcoves for Botany and for Zoölogy; from 50,000 to 100,000 it has alcoves for Birds, Fishes, Insects, Mammals, Reptiles, but it must be either very large or very special before it allows to smaller divisions of Zoölogy separate apartments. On an expansive system it is easy to make new alcoves as they are wanted; a similar multiplication by fission is possible in the successively enlarging editions of a printed catalogue. A card catalogue, designed for continuous growth, should have more thorough division than can be put into print, because it must look into the future, while the printed catalogue has no future.

As to (1) I can only say that the divisions of *Language* seem to me too intimately connected to be dispersed in catalogues of the present size, but that those of *Literature* have a more substantive existence and ought to be separated sooner. A double subdivision, however, ought to be avoided. Under *Language* there should be only one alphabet. It is better to arrange

	than
Greece. *Language.* *Accents.*	*Dictionaries.*
Dictionaries.	*Etymology.*
Ellipses.	*Grammar.*
Etymology.	*Accents.*
Grammar.	*Ellipses.*
History.	*Particles.*
Particles.	*Pleonasms.*
Pleonasms.	*Pronunciation.*
Pronunciation.	*Syntax.*
Syntax.	*History.*

Any subdivision of the groups under countries has been strongly opposed as being troublesome to make, useless and even confusing, or as being an unlawful mixture of classed and dictionary cataloguing. But suppose you have four or five hundred titles under **France.** *History.* Will you break them up into groups with such headings as *House of Bourbon, Revolution, Empire, Restoration, &c.*, with references and other devices for those works which treat of several periods, all of which it must be confessed is a little formidable at first glance, or will you leave them in one undivided mass, so that he who wants to find the history of the **last** half of the 15th century must read through the 500 titles perhaps to find even one and certainly to find all? You would divide of course. It is true that grouping may mislead. The inquirer must still be careful to look in several places. The history of France during the ascendency of the House of Valois is to be found not merely under that heading but in the comprehensive histories of the country. The inquirer is not less likely to think of this because the titles of these two groups are separated from the many other titles which have nothing to do specially or generally with the House of Valois, and if he does think of it he is greatly assisted by such segregation.

J. *Etc.*

203. In a supplement, catalogue the *whole* of a continued set, not merely the volumes received since the first catalogue.

But this should not be done when it will take up much space, as would often be the case with periodicals, owing to details of change of name, number of volumes missing, etc. Nor should Contents be repeated; it is enough to refer.

204. When there are many editions of a work under any subject-heading omit the titles and merely refer to the author-entry.

Much space may thus be saved at little inconvenience to the reader.

Ex. **Gaul.** CÆSAR, C. J. Commentarii [B.C. 58–49]. *See* **Cæsar**, C. J. (pp. 441, 442); here two lines do the work of forty.

205. Rare books.

American libraries and especially town libraries seldom have any books sufficiently rare to deserve great particularity of description. If for any reason it is thought necessary to give a minute account of a book or of a collection good models may be found in Trömel's Biblioth. amér., Lpz., 1861, 8°, Stevens's Historical nuggets, Lond., 1862, 2 v. 16°, Weller's Repertorium bibliographicum, Nördlingen, 1864, 8°, Harrisse's Biblioth. Amer. vetustissima, N. Y., 1866, 8°, Tiele's Mém. bibliog. sur les journaux des navig. néerlandaises, Amst., 1867, 8°, and the titles of the rarer books in Sabin's Dict. of books rel. to America, N. Y., 1868, etc. For the convenience of those who have not these works at hand a few examples are given here.

Leonardus *de Utino* or *de Belluno*. Sermones aurei de sanctis. [*Colophon:*] Expliciūt Sermones aurei | de sanctis per totū annum q̊ˢ | cōpilauit magister Leonar|dus de Vtino sacre theologie | doctor .... | Ad instantiam & cō|placentiā magnifice coītatis | Vtinensis ... | ... | .... M. cccc. xlvi. ... | ... | ... | ... | ... | [Coloniæ, *per Ulr. Zel,*]. M. cccc. Lxxiij. f°. Registr*um* (47) pp., (4) pp. blank, Tabula (1) p., (244) ll. In 2 coll. of 36 lines.

This copy has the leaves numbered in ms. and a Tabula prefixed to the 2d part by a contemporary hand. The work being very thick was probably in general bound in two parts and is rarely complete; Santander describes only the 1st part, the duc de la Vallière had only the 2d. The name of the printer, Zell, is found in only three or four of his numerous publications. This is shown to be his by the type, which is the same as that used in the Sermones of R. Caracciolus de Litio issued in the same year. The present work went through 10 editions in 8 years. According to Graesse it is probably the first printed out of Italy which contains a line of Italian poetry, "Trenta foglie ha la rosa" at the end of the 1st part.

Brunet v. 1022, Graesse VI. ii. 232, Hain no. 16128.

(47) pp. means 47 unnumbered pages, ll. means leaves.

Huon *de Bordeaux*. Les gestes et faictz | merueilleux du no|ble Huon de Bor-|deaulx .... Nouuellement redige en bon | Francoys: et Imprime nouuellement a Paris pour Jean Bonfonds | ... | ... | [*Ending*] Lequel liure ... a este mis de rime en prose | ... | ... | ... | ... | ... lequel fut fait & parfait le vinte | neufiesme iour de Januier. Lan | mil. cccc. liiii. ... | ... | ... | ... | ... | ... Imprime a Paris pour Jan | Bonfons. ... | ... *n.d.* 4°. (8), 264 ll. @ 40 lines. With 14 woodcuts in the text, and the printer's mark.

On the eighth leaf is written "Jehan Moynard me possidet 1557," which is probably not far from the date of publication. The 1st dated edition appeared in 1516. Brunet mentions two other editions before recording the present, one 1556, one undated.

Sold, Essling 95 *fr.*, Giraud 199 *fr.*

APPENDIX I.

So far we have been considering only the catalogue by which the library communicates with the public; but a librarian needs several others for library service: (1) The Catalogue of books ordered; (2) The Accessions-catalogue; (3) The Periodical- and continuation-book; (4) The Shelf-list; (5) The Catalogue of books missing; (6) The Tract-catalogue; (7) The Catalogue of duplicates to be sold; (8) The Catalogue of duplicates sold or exchanged.

(2) and (8) are necessary for the preservation of the history of the library and important in its financial management.

(6) is a modification of (5). It is a list of the tracts contained in bound volumes, by which the abstraction of any particular tract can be ascertained, or the extent of the loss if the whole volume disappears. All this might be entered on the shelf-list, but it is more convenient to keep the record of the tract volumes together. Sometimes part of a tract-list is inserted in the public catalogue. You may see collections of pamphlets on various subjects by various authors recorded under a made-up heading **Tracts**, or **Pamphlets**, a style of entry that is nearly useless. The whole of the Prince catalogue of 1846 was made in this absurd way. A number of tracts by a single author may indeed for economy be catalogued under him in one mass like a "contents," and the same may be done for tracts on a single subject, though there are objections even to this; but to catalogue the writings of several authors under an arbitrary heading (as **Plays, Speeches, French Revolution**), to which references merely are made under the authors, is to be economical at altogether too great an expense of trouble to the public,—to say nothing of the incongruity of a form or subject heading for an author-entry.

(4), the shelf-list, ought to be so made (*a*) that the entry of each book in the catalogue can be readily found from it; (*b*) that the book can be readily identified with the entry on the shelf-list; (*c*) that at the annual examination or taking account of stock the shelf-reader shall know at once what book is meant as each title is read by the list-reader. For these reasons the list should contain the author's name (or first-word, etc., if the book is anonymous), part of the real title, the binder's title (which will generally be the same as the real), and the place and date of printing. If the author's name, or any part of the title, is not on the back of the book it should be enclosed in parentheses.

Ex. Appuleius. Metamorphoses, tr. Head. L. 1851. 1
(Reinhardt. Artist's journey.) Bost. 1872. 1

A briefer shelf list can be made by merely entering the book's number and the accessions-number, so that the full title can be found if needed by referring to the accessions-book.

(2), (3), and (8) are best kept in books; (4) and (6) on separate sheets of paper; (1), (5), and (7) on cards. When the catalogue is kept on cards (5) can be made by merely separating the cards of such books as are missing.

(1). After some experiments I have preferred the following method of keeping the order-list. The titles of books proposed for purchase are written on ruled slips of stiff paper 5 in. long by 2 in. wide. If approved by the committee a check is made at the left of the title. A searcher then ascertains whether the library already has the book; if it has, the card is destroyed or sent with this information to the person who asked for the book; if not, the searcher puts her initials in the lower left-hand corner. The cards are then sorted into parcels for the English, French, or German agents; and an order is written, the writer first making sure, by looking among the cards of previous orders, that none of the books has already been sent for. In the order a running number is given to each title and a corresponding number is put on the card.

The name of the author is entered in a book opposite the running number, and the date is put there against the first number of each order.* The cards are then all stamped on the left with the date, and put away in a drawer alphabetically with other cards of books ordered. When a box of books comes, the corresponding cards are picked out and stamped on the right with the date. They receive the accessions-number when the books are entered on the accessions-catalogue, the shelf-number when the books are placed, and are corrected when the books are catalogued; for, having usually been written from advertisements, these cards are often incorrect. When a number have accumulated they are sorted in the order of shelf-numbers and the entry on the shelf-catalogue is made from them. They are then put away alphabetically in drawers accessible only to the library-attendants, and form the index of the accessions-book. When a duplicate volume is exchanged or sold the date, its price, and receiver are noted on the order-card.

The system is economical. One card serves many purposes and with little writing answers all the questions likely to come up: Has this book been proposed to the Book Committee? (Books rejected are kept in a separate drawer.) Has it been approved? Ordered? When? From whom? Who is responsible for the error if it turns out a duplicate? When was it received? Where is it entered in the Accessions-catalogue (that we may ascertain its price and condition)? Where was it first located? If any one of the questions is not to be asked then the corresponding process can be dispensed with. The list of which an example is given in the note below is not necessary but convenient.

[Specimen.]

Darwin, Charles.
39625 Coral Reefs. 2d ed. London, 1874. 8°.
19.41
2915 [Stamp, with date of order.] [Stamp, with date of receipt.]

---

*Jan. 1, 1875. 1497 Black.
1498 Hammond.
1499 Greville.
1500 Sanson.

APPENDIX II.

SOME WORKS OF REFERENCE.

I have set down here only those works which I find to be of *constant* use in cataloguing. One occasionally needs many more, even for a short investigation. A complete and systematic view of bibliographical literature is given in Petzholdt's "Bibliotheca bibliographica. Leipzig, 1866." Powers' "Handy-book about books. London, 1870," contains a useful list, which is reprinted, with additions, in Sabin's "American bibliopolist."

BALLHORN. Grammatography. Lond., 1861. 8°. 7*s.* 6*d.*

BRUNET. Manuel. 5e éd. Paris, 1860–65. 6 v. 8°. 120*fr.*

HŒFER. Nouvelle biographie générale. Paris, 1852–66. 46 v. 8°. 184*fr.*

HORNE. Introd. to bibliography. Lond., 1814. 2 v. 8°. *Antiq.* 18*s.*

JOECHER. Allgem. Gelehrten-Lexikon. Lpz., 1850–51. 4 v. 4°, and Fortsetzung. Bremen, 1784–1819. 6 v. 4°. *Antiq.* 40 *fl.*

LAROUSSE. Dictionnaire universel Paris, 1866–76. 15 v. 8°. 518*fr.*

MEN of the time. 8th ed. London, 1872. 12*s.* 6*d.*

MICHAELIS. Vergleichendes Wörterbuch der gebräuchlichsten Taufnamen. Berl., 1856. 8°. 15 *Ngr.*

OETTINGER. Moniteur des dates. Dresde, 1866–68. 6 v. 4°. 35 *Thlr.* (Supplement now publishing.)

THOMAS. Universal dict. of biog. and mythol. Phila., 1870. 2 v. 8°. $22 or 1 v. $15.

TOWNSEND. Manual of dates. 3d ed. Lond., 1869. 8°. 18*s.*

VAPEREAU. Dict. des contemporains. 4e éd. Paris, 1870. 8°. 25*fr.*

AMERICAN.

ALLIBONE. Dict. of Eng. literature. Phila., 1858–71. 3 v. 8°. $22.50.

DRAKE. Dict. of Amer. biog. Rev. ed. Bost., 1875. 8°. $6.

HARRISSE. Biblioth. Amer. vetustissima; works rel. to Amer. pub. 1492–1551. N. Y., 1866. 8°. $20.

LEYPOLDT. Amer. catalogue. N. Y. Announced for 1876. $25.

SABIN. Dict. of books rel. to Amer. N. Y., 1868, etc. 4°. $5 per vol.

SPRAGUE. Annals of the American pulpit. N. Y., 1857–69. 9 v. 8°. $36.

The following may sometimes be of use: ROORBACH'S Biblioth Amer., 1820–61. 4 v. 8°, and KELLY'S Amer. catalogue, 1861–71. N. Y., 1866–71. 2 v. 8°

ART.

POLLEN. Universal catal. of books on art. Lond., 1868–70. 2 v. Sm. 4°. 21*s.*

DUTCH.

KOBUS *and* RIVECOURT. Biog. handwoordenboek. Zutphen, 1854–61. 3 v. 8°. About $4.

Convenient; for fuller details use

AA. Biog. woord. [A–O]. Haarlem, 1852–67. 14 v. 8°.

ENGLISH.

ALLIBONE. Dict. of Eng. literature. Phila., 1858–71. 3 v. 8°. $22.50.
BURKE. Peerage and baronetage. 38th ed. Lond., 1876? 8°. 38*s.*
BURKE. Dormant and extinct peerages. New ed. Lond., 1866. 8°. 42*s.*
COLLIER. Bibliog. account of the rarest works in English. Lond., 1868. 2 v. 8°, or N. Y., 1868. 2 v. 8°. $16.
DARLING. Cyclopædia bibliog.: Authors. Lond., 1854. 8°. 52*s.* 6*d.*
Chiefly English theol. works.
HAYDN. Book of dignities. Lond., 1851. 8°. 25*s.*
LOWNDES. Bibliog. manual of Eng. literature. New ed., enl. by H. G. Bohn. Lond., 1857–64. 6 v. 8°. 33*s.*
NICOLAS. Historic peerage. Lond., 1857. 8°. 30*s.*
ROSSE. Index of dates. Lond., *Bohn*, 1858. 2 v. 8°. $2.50.
THOMAS. Handbook of fictitious names; by Olphar Hamst [pseud.]. Lond., 1868. 8°. 7*s.* 6*d.*
WALFORD. County families of Gr. Brit. New ed. Lond., 1874. 8°. 50*s.*
WATT. Bibliotheca Britannica. Edin., 1824. 4 v. 4°. *Antiq.* £4 15*s.*

The following may sometimes be of use: Low's English catalogue, 1835–71. Lond., 1864–73. 2 v. 8°. 75*s.*, and Low's [Subject] index to the British catalogue, 1837–57. Lond., 1858. 8°. 26*s.* Vol. 2, 1857, etc., is in preparation.

FRENCH.

BARBIER. Ouvrages anonymes. 3e éd. Paris, 1872–76? 3 v. 8°. 60 *fr.*
LORENZ. Catal. gén. de la librairie française, 1840–65. Paris, 1867–71. 4 v. 8°. 100 *fr.*
QUÉRARD. La France littéraire. Paris, 1827–39. 10 v. 8°. 120 *fr.*
QUÉRARD. Supercheries littéraires. 2e éd. Paris, 1869–70. 3 v. 8°. 60 *fr.*
QUÉRARD *and others.* La littérature française contemporaine. Paris, 1842–57. 6 v. 8°. 96 *fr.*

GERMAN.

HEINSIUS. Allgem. Bücher-Lexikon; Verzeichniss aller von 1700 bis 1874 erschienenen Bücher. Lpz., 1812–75. 15 v. 4°.
KAYSER. Vollständ. Bücher-Lexicon, 1750–1870. Lpz., 1834–73. 18 v. 4°. About $60.

GREEK AND ROMAN.

SMITH. Dict. of Gr. and Rom. biography and mythology. Lond., 1849. 3 v. 8°. 115*s.* 6*d.*, or Bost. $30.

HEBREW.

BRITISH MUSEUM. Catal. of Hebr. books. Lond., 1867. 8°. 25*s.*
FUERST. Biblioth. Judaica. Lpz., 1849–63. 3 v. 8°. 14 *Thlr.*

INCUNABULA.

BERJEAU. Early German, Dutch, and English printers' marks. Lond., 1866. 8°. 10*s.* 6*d.*

HAIN. Repertorium bibliogr. Stüttg., 1826–38. 2 v. 8°. 20 *Thlr.*
PANZER. Annales typogr., 1457–1536. Norimb., 1793–1803. 11 v. 4°. *Antiq.* 42 *Thlr.*

ITALIAN

MELZI. Diz. di opere anon. e pseud. Milano, 1848–59. 3 v. 8°. 30 *fr.*
TIRABOSCHI. Storia della lit. ital. Mil., 1822–26. 16 v. 8°.

LANGUAGE.

VATER. Litteratur der Grammatiken, Lexika, *u.s.w.* 2e Aufl. Berl. 1847. 8°. 3 *Thlr.*

MEDIÆVAL.

CHASSANT. Dict. des abréviations lat. et françaises. 3e éd. Paris, 1866. 16°. 6 *fr.*
GRAESSE. Orbis Latinus; Verzeichniss d. latein. Benennungen der Städte, *u.s.w.* Dresden, 1861. 8°. 1½ *Thlr.*
POTTHAST. Biblioth. historica Medii Ævi. Berlin, 1862. 8°, and supplement, 1868. 9 *Thlr.*

MUSICIANS.

FÉTIS. Biog. univ. des musiciens. 2e éd. augm. Paris, 1860–65. 8 v. 8°. 64 *fr.*

QUAKERS.

SMITH. Biblioth. anti-Quakerana. Lond., 1873. 8°. 15*s.*
SMITH. Descr. catal. of Friends' books. Lond., 1867. 2 v. 8°.

SCIENCE.

POGGENDORF. Biog.-lit. Handwörterbuch zur Gesch. d. exacten Wissenschaften. Lpz., 1863. 2 v. 8°. 10⅔ *Thlr.*
ROYAL SOCIETY OF LONDON. Catal. of scientific papers, 1800–63. Lond., 1867–72. 6 v. 4°. £6.

SPANISH.

ANTONIO. Bibliotheca Hispana vetus, ad a. C. MD. Matriti, 1788. 2 v. f°. *Antiq.* 40 à 50 *fr.*
— *Same.* Nova, 1500–1684. Matriti, 1783–88. 2 v. f°. *Antiq.* 40 à 50 *fr.*
TICKNOR. Hist. of Span. lit. 4th ed. Bost., 1872. 3 v. 8°. $10.

WOMEN.

HALE. Woman's record. N. Y., 1853. 8°. $5.

ADDENDUM.

FRANKLIN, A. Dict. des noms, surnoms, et pseudonymes latins, 1100–1530. Paris, 1875. 8°. 10 *fr.*

INDEX.

The figures preceded by p. *refer to the pages; the others to the sections.*

Abbot, Ezra, p. 5.
Abbreviations, 116, 138; arrangement of, 185.
Abridgement, 110–119.
Academies, 40.
Accents, 164.
Accessions-catalogue, p. 81.
Acts of legislative bodies, 28.
Almanacs, 54.
Alternative titles, 121, 161.
American, how used, p. 45.
Analytical references defined, p. 15; when to be made, 49, 78, 91–93, 124; arrangement of, 193.
Annuals, 54.
Anonymous defined, p. 10.
Anonymous books, 1, 39, 52, 53, 61–63, 130, 131.
Appended, 153.
Apprentices' Library, N. Y., p. 5.
Arabic numerals, 117, 145, 149.
Arabic writers, 13 *e*; transliteration of Arabic names, 25.
Arrangement, 169–202.
Articles, 56, 110, 111; place of, when transposed, 129; initial, not noticed in arrangement, 187.
Articles to be inquired of, 31.
Associations, 40.
Asyndetic, p. 10.
Auctioneers, 8.
Author defined, p. 10.
Author-entry, p. 14, § 1–31, 92 *c*.

Bible, 52; arrangement of titles under, 196.
Bibliography, 83.
Binder's-title, p. 15. § 153.
Biographies, economy in the entry of, 51; anonymous, 52, 62; of kings, etc., 67; arrangement of, 191.
Booksellers, 8.
Brackets, 165, 166.
Breviaries, 35.
British Museum, p. 5.
Buildings, 40.

Canonized persons, 13 *b*, 44.
Capes, 19.
Capitals, 161, 162.
Caption, p. 15.
Catalogue of accessions, of books ordered, of books missing, etc., p. 81.
Catalogues, how entered, 8.
Catalogues, table of the different kinds, p. 13.
Cataloguing, list of books useful in, p. 83.
Catch-word-entry, p. 14; reference, p. 15.
Catch-word-reference, 61.
Catechisms, 35.
Changed names, 15, 44.
Charges, episcopal, 31.
Christian names, 13, 94, 103, 104, 115, 171, 172.
Chronograms, 145.
Chronological arrangement, 200.
Churches, 35, 40.
Cities, 27; cross-references from, 85.
Civil actions, 81.
Class defined, p. 10; its relation to subject, p. 12.
Class-entry, p. 12.
Classed catalogues, p. 12, 13.
Classes of citizens, 39.
Classes of persons, cross-references from, 85.
Classification, pp. 5, 10–12, 47.
Collectors, 43.
Colleges, 40.
Colophon, 142.
Commentaries, 9, 44.
Comments, 82.
Committees, 38.
Composers of music, 7.
Compound headings, 76.
Compound names, 16, 44, 179–183.
Concordances, 11.
Conferences, 36.
Confessions of faith, 35.
Congress, 28.
Congresses, 33, 44.
Contents, 155–157, 168; arrangement of, 197.
Continuations, 10, 44.
Conventions, 36, 44.
Corporate-entry, 26–40.
Councils, ecclesiastical, 37, 44.
Country and person, choice between, 67.
Country and subject, 68.
Countries as joint authors, 2; cross-references from, 85; arrangement under, 194–196.
Courts, 27.
Creeds, 35.
Criticisms, 192; of anonymous works, 53.
Cross-reference, p. 15, § 85, 86, 201.

D', de, de la, des, du, 17.
Daily, 57.
Danish names, 25.
Dashes, 107.
Date of publication, 142–152.
Dates, 114.
Defendant of a thesis, 4, 44.
Definitions of terms used in cataloguing, p. 10.
Denominations, 34.
Designers, 6, 6½, 44.
Dictionaries, 90.
Dictionary catalogues defined, p. 12.
Dictionary and systematic catalogues, p. 47.
Directories, 47.
Divisions, 202.

Divorced wives, 14 *c*, 44.
Double-entry, 66, 67, 67½, 77–79.
Double title-pages, 65.
Drama, 88.
Dutch names, 25.

Ecclesiastical councils, 37, 44; dignitaries, 14 *b*, 44; districts, 27.
Economies in author-entry, 46–51; in subject-entry, p. 39 *d*, 45 *k*, § 67, 68, 79½, 80, 81, 204.
Editions, 119, 134, 135; arrangement of, 188.
Editor, p. 10, § 11, 101; of periodicals, 42–44, 54.
Editors, 101.
Encyclopædias, p. 14, § 90.
Engravings, 6, 6½, 44.
Entry defined, p. 14; where to enter, § 1–93; how to enter, 94–205.
Episcopal charges, 31.
Epitomes, 10.
Eschatology, 84.
Essays, 92 *d*.
Evening, 57.
Events, 67½.
Exact copying, 125.

Family name, 102.
Fiction, 55.
Firms, 40.
First-word, what it is, 56–58.
First-word-entry, p. 14.
First-word reference, p. 15, § 59, 60.
First-words, 98, 122.
Form, p. 14.
Form, typographical, 154.
Form-entry, p. 14, § 88; classification by, p. 11.
Forts, 19.
Friars, 13 *c*, 44.
Full defined, p. 9.
Future life, 84.

Galleries, 40.
Gazetteers, 47.
German names, 25.
Governmental bodies, publications of, 28, 195; references from governmental publications, 64.
Grammars, 90.
Greek names, ancient and modern, 25; ancient, 178.
Greek names of deities, 70.
Guilds, 40.

Half-title, p. 15.
Harris, Wm. T., p. 5.
Harvard College Library, p. 5.
Heading, p. 14.
Heading reference, p. 15.
Headings, style of, 94–108; arrangement of, 170–185.
Historical societies, 40.
Homonyms, 75, 198.
Hungarian names, 25.
Huon de Bordeaux, 205.
Hyphened words, 183.

Illustrators, 6, 44.
Immortality, 84.
Important-word-entry, p. 14.
Imprint, p. 14, § 136–154.
Incunabula, 205.
Indexes, 10, 44, 90.
Individual subjects, p. 12.
Initials, 44, 115; entry under, 41; for Christian names, 103; for the subject-heading, 118.
Introductions, 44 (10).
Inversion of subject-names, 76.
Italics, 95, 167, 168.

Jewett, C. C., p. 5.
Jewish writers, 13 *e*.
Joint authors, 2, 3, 44, 93, 186.
Journals of legislative bodies, 28; of conventions, *etc.*, 36; of societies, 40.

Kings, works written by, 27, 30; works about, 67.

L', la, le, 17.
Lakes, 19.
Language, classification by, p. 11.
Language of a book to be stated in the title, 126, 127.
Language of subject-names, 70.
Latin names, 18, 44, 178.
Latin names of Greek deities, 70.
Latinized form of Greek names, 25.
Laws, 28, 29.
Leonardus de Utino, 205.
Libraries, 40.
Literary form, p. 14.
Literary history, 83.
Liturgies, 35.

M', Mc, *etc.*, 173.
Manifestoes, 35.
Married women, 14 *c*, 44.
Mediæval works, 52.
Medium defined, p. 9.
Memoirs of societies, 40, 54; their subject-entry, p. 37.
Mercantile library associations, 40.
Minerals, 189.
Minutes of legislative bodies, 28; of conventions, 33.
Missals, 35.
Morning, 57.
Mottoes, 122.
Mountains, 19.
Museums, 40.
Musical works, 7.

Name, under what part of the, the entry should be made, 13–25; entry under parts of a, 41, 44.
Names of subjects, 70–79.
Nichols, Th., p. 5.
Noblemen, 14 *b*, 44.
Notes, 158.
Novels, 55, 88.
Numbers, 117.
Numerals, initial, disregarded in arrangement, 189.

Objects of a dictionary-catalogue, p. 10.
Official writings, entry of, 30.
Omissions. *See* Abridgement.
Order of the parts of an imprint, 136; of the parts of an entry, 163.

Order of the title to be preserved, 109.
Order-list, p. 81.
Orders, military and religious, 35.
Oriental authors, 13 *e*, 44.

Pages, number of, 136, 152.
Parentheses, 134, 165, 166.
Parliament, 28.
Parties, 34, 35.
Periodicals, 54.
Periods in history, 67½.
Perkins, F. B., p. 5.
Person and country, choice between, 67.
Personal names, 1–25.
Place, entry of that part of a body which belongs to a, 35.
Place of publication, 137–140, 142, 147.
Places, names of, 22–24; entry under, 27, 40; compound names of, 180.
Platforms, 35.
Plays, 59, 88.
Poems, 59.
Poetry, 88.
Polygraphic, p. 14.
Polytopical, p. 14.
Position, 118.
Possessive case, 177
Practical form, p. 14.
Praeses, 4, 44.
Prayer books, 35.
Prefixes to names, 17, 44, 173, 179.
Prepositions, 56.
Presidential conventions, 26.
Princes, 13 *a*, 44.
Proceedings, 40, 54; their subject-entry, p. 37.
Proper names, 161, 162.
Pseudonyms, entry under, 5, 42, 44; arrangement of, 184; the use of *pseud.*, 99, 100.
Publication, place of, 137–140, 142, 147.
Publishers, 141.
Publishing societies, 43 *d*.
Punctuation, 163.

Rare books, 205.
Reference, p. 14, 108, 159, 160; author-references, 44, 45, 46.
References, 159, 160.
Registers, 47.
Reigns, histories of, 67.
Reporters, 11, 48.
Reports, how entered, 32; governmental, 28; of committees, 38; of conventions, conferences, etc., 36.
Respondent of a thesis, 4, 44.
Reviews, 82, 92.
Rivers, 19.
Romaic names, 25.

St. Louis Public School Library, p. 5.
Saints, 13 *b*, 44.
Same, 119.
Schools, 40.
Schwartz, J., p. 5.
See and *See also*, 159, 167.
Serials, 54.
Sets of works, 92.
Shelf-catalogue, p. 81.
Short defined, p. 9.
Size or typographical form, 154.
Societies, 40, 92; references to works entered under the names of, 64; names of, how arranged, 182.
Sovereigns, 13 *a*, 44.
Spanish names, 25.
Specific entry, p. 13, 15, § 66.
Spelling, variety of, 21, 44, 58.
Style of entry, 94–205.
Subarrangement, chronological, 200.
Subdivisions under countries, 68, 76 (end of note), 195; under other subjects, 199–202.
Subject defined, p. 15; classification by, p. 11; its relation to class, p. 12.
Subject and country, choice between, 68.
Subject-entry, p. 14, § 66–87, 92 *b*.
Subject-word and subject, 74.
Subject-word-entry, p. 14, § 62; reference, p. 15, § 63.
Subjects, arrangement of, 198–202.
Supplements, 203.
Surnames, 14.
Swedish names, 25.
Syndetic, p. 15.
Synonymous subject-names, 71–73.
Synoptical table, 87.
Systematic and dictionary catalogues, p. 47.

Theses, 4, 44.
Title defined, p. 15; its influence on entry, p. 16, § 1, 2, 74.
Title-entry, p. 14, § 52.
Title-pages, double, 65.
Title references, 59–64.
Titles, style of, 109–133; arrangement of, 186–196.
Titles of honor to be italicized in headings, 95; and not in titles, 132; capitals for, 161, 162; arrangement of, 176.
Towns, 27.
Transactions of societies, 40, 54; their subject-entry, p. 57.
Translations, 127, 128; arrangement of, 190.
Translations of anonymous works, 53.
Translators, 11, 44 (42).
Transliteration, 25, 133, 137.
Treaties, 34.
Trials, 48, 81.
Type, 94–98.
Typographical form, 154.

Uniformity, p. 53.
Universities, 40.

Van, von, 17.
Vernacular to be used in spelling, 20.
Vessels, 48, 80.
Volume defined, p. 16.
Volumes, number of, 153.

Weekly, 57.

Young men's Christian associations, 40.

www.ingramcontent.com/pod-product-compliance
Lightning Source LLC
LaVergne TN
LVHW011119110826
845150LV00008B/2183
* 9 7 8 1 4 2 5 5 7 1 9 8 6 *